COUNTERFEIT
OR
GENUINE?
Mark 16? John 8?

Books by David Otis Fuller

Which Bible?
True or False?
Treasury of Evangelical Writings
Counterfeit or Genuine? —
    Mark 16? John 8?

COUNTERFEIT
OR
GENUINE?
Mark 16? John 8?

Edited by

David Otis Fuller, D.D.

Grand Rapids International Publications
Grand Rapids, Michigan 49501

Library of Congress Cataloging Card Number: 74-82807

ISBN 0-8254-2615-4

4 5 6 7 8 printing/year 95 94 93 92 91 90

Printed in the United States of America

DEDICATED TO

Jasper James Ray, Missionary Scholar of Junction City, Oregon, whose book, *God Wrote Only One Bible,* moved me to begin this fascinating, faith-inspiring study

Sincere appreciation to Linda Blunt, my very efficient secretary, who put the original manuscript into shape in record time.

My deepest thanks to Donald Waite, Ph.D., Th.D., who gave me the idea and urged me over the telephone while I was hospitalized to condense this masterpiece of John Burgon.

CONTENTS

INTRODUCTION

The compiler of this masterpiece by John W. Burgon is convinced beyond any question of one thing: born-again Christians in this twentieth century are facing the most malicious and vicious attack upon God's inspired Holy Word since the Garden of Eden. And this attack began in its modern form in the publication of the Revised Version of the Scriptures in 1881 in England.

For the above statement there is abundant evidence found in two volumes, *Which Bible?* (now in its tenth edition) and *True or False?* with a combined total of over six hundred pages containing documentary proof that, in the editor's estimation, is irrefutable. *

Furthermore, if we as Christians, saved by the sovereign grace of God and the precious blood of Christ, His eternal Son, do not have an infallible, inspired, inerrant Word of God to rest our weary souls upon for Time and Eternity, then we are of all men most miserable and our salvation is worth nothing. With John Wesley we are at one when he says: "I build on no authority, ancient or modern, but the Scripture. I want to know one thing—the way to heaven; how to land safe on that happy shore. God Himself hath condescended to teach the Way, He hath written it down in a Book. Oh give me that Book! At any price, give me that Book of God!"

In the Revised Version of 1881 a number of passages in God's Word are called in question; grave doubts are cast upon them when the footnotes tell us that "the oldest and best manuscripts" omit them. By "oldest and best"

*Both books edited by Dr. Fuller and available from Kregel Publications, Grand Rapids, Michigan 49501.

Westcott and Hort and the other translators, except for Prebendary Scrivener, meant primarily Codex B (or Vaticanus) and Codex Aleph (or Sinaiticus). Both of these manuscripts were the oldest, but there is overwhelming proof they are the poorest and most unreliable.

The longest passage called in question by Westcott and Hort and Bishop Ellicott—who dominated, domineered, and engineered the proceedings from beginning to end—is Mark 16:9-20. Dean Burgon has proceeded to provide thoroughly documented proof that this section of God's Holy Word was in the original autographs. This is found in this condensed volume of his original work, which consisted of well over four hundred pages and was one of the most scholarly, carefully documented critiques that has ever been written on this subject and one that no scholar has ever answered or even attempted to answer.

Other passages called in question by the Revised Version of 1881 in the footnotes, to name a few, are John 7:53 to 8:11; Acts 8:37; John 5:4; I Timothy 3:16; and I John 5:7. There are many more. There would have to be more when one realizes that the Revisers of 1881, led and coerced by this triumvirate of Westcott, Hort, and Ellicott, made well over thirty thousand changes of words and phrases from the King James Version, in some cases causing the real meaning of the passage to be changed completely or eliminated. One scholar who made a thorough study of the two versions came to the conclusion that 80 percent of the changes were entirely unnecessary.

Since the time of the Revised Version nearly one hundred versions of Scripture have been published; a few are good, but for the most part they are Perversions, vagrant versions, and in some cases just plain bastard Bibles. If the reader thinks the latter term too harsh, will he compare Psalm 22:16 in The New English Bible with the King James Version (KJV), or I Samuel 20:30 in the Living Bible with the KJV, or Zechariah 13:6 in The Living Bible with the same in the KJV. These are but a few of the terrible liberties being taken with God's inerrant Holy Word.

Knowing these things as we do, though not nearly as conversant with them as many others, I would be criminally culpable if I knowingly "held down the truth in unrighteousness" when it is my bounden duty to expose this terrible assault upon the sacred Scriptures. "To sin by silence when they should protest makes cowards of men." So spoke one of our greatest presidents, Abraham Lincoln; and we gladly echo his words.

Dean Burgon consistently refused to accept the word or opinion of this scholar or that one unless it was backed by demonstrable facts. So often Burgon discovered that scholars quoted other scholars without investigating their findings. Without any hesitation I maintain that John Burgon was one of the greatest scholars of the last century (being ranked by others with Tregelles, Tischendorf, and Scrivener). Proof for that is found in the British Museum. It was the privilege of this compiler, after struggling through several rounds of red tape, to see for myself three of the sixteen folio volumes Burgon had written in his own hand, a compilation of eighty-seven thousand quotations from the early Church Fathers. I make bold to say there is no other collection like this in existence.

In condensing the book by Burgon on Mark 16:9-20 we were amazed beyond words at the profundity of his vast research and very apparent scholarship. Even those who radically opposed his defense of the Sacred Text readily agreed to his erudition and great learning. Burgon agreed that the King James Version could and should have changes made to enhance the meaning of certain words and eliminate archaisms, but he fiercely opposed all who would slavishly follow in abject servility the Westcott and Hort Greek Text or their theory, which had and has no foundation whatever on which to stand.

Herman C. Hoskier was the understudy of John Burgon. His scholarship is of the highest caliber. His research, his painstaking study of manuscripts, and the text itself is clearly shown in the volumes he produced, now long out of print. We would challenge any contemporary scholar to produce a work similar to two of Hoskier's volumes on the four Gospels, each four hundred pages in length. Hoskier's book *Codex B and Its Allies—A Study and an Indictment* is quoted in large part in *Which Bible?* He has marshaled a vast amount of documentary evidence in a volume of nearly five hundred pages, clearly demonstrating the utter unreliability of the group of manuscripts headed by Codex Vaticanus (or B) and Codex Sinaiticus (or Aleph), which were held in such high esteem by Professors Westcott and

Hort and a multitude of scholars since, and are so held today, by those who have "followed in their train."

On one occasion Hoskier reported: "Three and a half years ago [this was written in 1890] I was in Dean Burgon's study at Chichester. It was midnight, dark and cold without; he had just extinguished the lights, and it was dark, and getting cold within. We mounted the stairs to retire to rest, and his last words of the night have often rung in my ears since: 'As surely as it is dark now, and as certainly as the sun will rise tomorrow morning, so surely will the Traditional Text be vindicated and the views I have striven to express be accepted. I may not live to see it. Most likely I shall not. But it will come!' "

This is a David and Goliath battle with practically all of the evangelical seminaries and colleges, Bible institutes, and Bible schools slavishly following essentially the Westcott and Hort Greek Text and the Westcott and Hort theory, both of which are fallacious in every particular, the former based on two of the worst manuscripts, the latter proven to be without foundation of any kind.

All of this tells the born-again Christian a very simple but pointed truth. Christians need to divorce themselves from the television set and spend at least half as much time studying this intensely fascinating and important subject. Any layman, with no knowledge of Greek or Hebrew (or indeed any other language but English), can secure a sound comprehension of the issues involved and thus declare with authority the fact that God has not only inspired "holy men of old" to write His very words—without affecting their own style of writing or personalities—but He also has kept His Word intact, pure, and without error down through the centuries. Among the nearly one hundred versions available to today's readers, the one that is nearest to the original autographs is the King James Version. We repeat: Changes could and should be made to enhance the meaning, but as Burgon has so convincingly shown in this book, neither Mark 16:9-20 nor any other verse or verses need to be deleted for a moment. All sixty-six books, all 1,189 chapters, and all 29,921 verses are God's inspired Word.

David Otis Fuller

THE MAGNIFICENT BURGON

Edward F. Hills, A.B., Th.D.

THE MAGNIFICENT BURGON

Dean Burgon and the Traditional Text

Every faithful Christian must reckon seriously with the teaching of Christ concerning the providential preservation of Scripture. Our Lord evidently believed that the Old Testament Scriptures had been preserved in their original purity from the time of their first writing down to His own day and that this providential preservation would continue until the end of the ages.

There are two passages especially which clearly indicate this. The first is Matthew 5:18, "Till heaven and earth pass away, one jot or one tittle shall in no wise pass from the law until all be fulfilled." The second is Luke 16:17, "It is easier for heaven and earth to pass away, then one tittle of the law to fail." Here Jesus attributes greater stability to the text of the Old Testament than to the heavens and earth. Calvin has well explained these words of Christ: "There is nothing in the law that is unimportant, nothing that was put there at random; and so it is impossible that a single letter shall perish."

Christ also promised that the same Divine providence which had preserved the Old Testament would preserve the New Testament too. In the concluding verses of the Gospel of Matthew we find His "Great Commission" not only to the twelve apostles but also to His Church throughout all ages, "go ye therefore and teach all nations." Implied in this solemn charge is the promise that through the working

of God's providence the Church will always be kept in
possession of an infallible record of Christ's words and
works.

And, similarly, in His discourses on the last things He
assures His disciples that His words not only will certainly
be fulfilled but will remain available for the comfort of His
people during that troubled period which will precede His
second coming. In other words, they will be preserved
until that time. "Heaven and earth shall pass away, but my
words shall not pass away" (Matt. 24:35; Mark 13:31;
Luke 21:33). Likewise, the Word of Christ is to be the
foundation of Christian character down through the ages
(Matt. 8:24-27) and the standard by which all men will be
judged at the last day (John 12:48).

Clearly, Christ promises that a trustworthy text of the
sacred New Testament books will be preserved in His
Church down through the ages until the last days. How has
this promise been fulfilled? By what special working of His
Divine providence has Christ kept this promise? Many
scholars have endeavored to answer this question, but none
have succeeded better than J. W. Burgon (1813-1888),
Dean of Chichester. The following paragraphs present a
summary of Burgon's views concerning the New Testament
text.

Most of Burgon's adult life was spent at Oxford, as
Fellow of Oriel College and then as vicar of St. Mary's (the
University Church) and Gresham Professor of Divinity.
During his last twelve years he was Dean of Chichester. His
father was an English merchant living in Turkey; and his
mother was a native of Smyrna, with an Austrian and
Greek ancestry.

It was from this foreign blood, no doubt, that Burgon
derived his warm and enthusiastic nature (not typically
English), which expressed itself in a lively literary style. In
theology he was a High Church Anglican, strenuously
upholding the doctrine of baptismal regeneration but
opposing the ritualism into which even in his day the High
Church movement had begun to decline. Throughout his
life he remained unmarried; but, like many other celibates,
he is said to have been unusually fond of children. As for
his learning, even his adversaries acknowledged that it was
very great.

The thing about Burgon, however, which lifts him out

of his nineteenth century English setting and endears him to the hearts of earnest Christians of other lands and ages is his steadfast defense of the Scriptures as the infallible Word of God. He strove with all his power to arrest the modernistic currents which during his lifetime had begun to flow within the Church of England, continuing his efforts with unabated zeal up to the very day of his death.

With this purpose in mind he labored mightily in the field of New Testament textual criticism. In 1860, while temporary chaplain of the English congregation at Rome, he made a personal examination of Codex B, and in 1862 he inspected the treasures of St. Catherine's Convent on Mt. Sinai. Later he made several tours of European libraries, examining and collating New Testament manuscripts wherever he went.

It is on the strength of these labors that K.W. Clark (1950) ranks him with Tregelles and Scrivener as one of the "great contemporaries" of Tischendorf. And Rendel Harris (1908) had high praise for Burgon's great index of New Testament quotations in the Church Fathers, which was deposited in the British Museum at the time of his death but has never been published. "It is possible," Harris said, "to object to many of his references and to find fault with some of the texts which he used, but I only wish that I possessed a transcript of these precious volumes."

Burgon was amassing all these materials for a definitive work in which he would defend the Traditional Text. This was Burgon's name for that type of text which is found in the vast majority of the extant Greek New Testament manuscripts, which was adopted by Protestants at the time of the Reformation and used by them universally for more than three hundred years, and which forms the basis of the King James Version and other early Protestant translations.

Unfortunately, however, Burgon did not live to complete his project. The fragments of it that he left at his death were pieced together by his friend E. Miller. These were published in 1896 in two volumes entitled *The Traditional Text of the Holy Gospels* and *The Causes of the Corruption of the Traditional Text.* The fact that Burgon died before he could finish his *magnum opus* is a matter of deep regret; but enough of it survives in Miller's volumes to convey to us Burgon's fundamental ideas, together with the arguments by which he supported them. And these same basic concepts had been expressed in two earlier books which had won him fame as a textual critic, namely, *The Last Twelve Verses of Mark* (1871), a defense of this portion of the New Testament text, and *The Revision Revised* (1883), a reprint of three articles in the *Quarterly Review* against the Revised Version of 1881, together with a reply to a pamphlet by Bishop Ellicott against these three articles. Such, then, were the publications in which Burgon laid down the principles of consistently Christian New Testament textual criticism and elaborated them with considerable fullness. Of all the great textual critics of the nineteenth century, Burgon alone was consistently Christian.

Dean Burgon the Champion of the Traditional (Byzantine) Text

According to Kenyon (1940), there are about 4,489 extant Greek New Testament manuscripts. Of these, 170 are papyrus fragments, dating from the second century to the seventh; 212 are uncial (capital letter) manuscripts, dating from the fourth century to the tenth; 2,429 are minuscule (small letter) manuscripts dating from the ninth century to the sixteenth; and 1,678 are lectionaries (lesson books for public reading containing extracts from the New Testament).

The vast majority of these extant Greek New Testament manuscripts agree together very closely—so closely, indeed, that they may fairly be said to contain the same New Testament text. This majority text is usually called the Byzantine text by modern textual critics. This is because all modern critics acknowledge that this was the Greek New Testament text in general use throughout the greater part of the Byzantine Period (312-1453).

For many centuries before the Protestant Reformation this Byzantine text was the text of the entire Greek Church, and for more than three centuries after the Reformation it was the text of the entire Protestant Church. Even today it is the text which most Protestants know best, since the King James Version and other early Protestant translations were made from it.

Burgon was an ardent defender of this Byzantine text found in the vast majority of the Greek New Testament manuscripts. He gave to this text the name Traditional Text, thus indicating his conviction that this was the true text which by a perpetual tradition had been handed down generation after generation without fail in the Church of Christ from the days of the apostles onward. Burgon believed this because he believed that it was through the Church that Christ had fulfilled His promise always to preserve for His people a true New Testament text.

The Byzantine text, Burgon maintained, is the true text because it is that form of the Greek New Testament which is known to have been used in the Church of Christ in unbroken succession for many centuries, first in the Greek Church and then in the Protestant Church. And all orthodox Christians, all Christians who show due regard for the Divine inspiration and providential preservation of Scripture, must agree with Burgon in this matter. For in what other way can it be that Christ has fulfilled His promise always to preserve in His Church the true New Testament text?

Burgon's reconstruction of the history of the New Testament text is not only vividly expressed but eminently Biblical and therefore true. For if the true New Testament text came from God, where did the erroneous variant readings ultimately come save from the evil one? And how could the true text have been preserved save through the providence of God working through His Church? No doubt most Christians, not being High Church Anglicans, will place less emphasis than Dean Burgon did on the organized Church and more emphasis on the providence of God working through the Church, especially the Greek Church. But this possible defect in Burgon's presentation does not in any essential way affect the unending validity of his views concerning the New Testament text. They are timeless because they are consistently Christian. In elaborating these views, Burgon, unlike most other textual critics, was always careful to remember that the New Testament is not an ordinary book but a special book—a book written under the infallible inspiration of the Holy Spirit, whose text Christ has promised to preserve in His Church down through the ages.

The Canon and Text of the New Testament

The essential soundness of Burgon's views is most

readily seen when we compare the history of the New
Testament canon with the history of the New Testament
text. Therefore, it is to this task that we must now address
ourselves.

Why did the Christian Church receive the twenty-seven
New Testament books and these only as her canonical New
Testament Scripture? Harnack (1914) and other noted
students of the New Testament canon have asked this
question repeatedly and have endeavored to answer it in
their own fashion. But, as Greijdanus (1927) and
Grosheide (1935) point out, this question can be satisfactorily answered only on the basis of Christian faith.
And when we look with the eye of faith on the history of
the New Testament canon, we see in that history a mighty
conflict between God and Satan, between the Holy Spirit
on the one hand and the Spirit of Darkness on the other.

First God gave His Church the twenty-seven New Testament books through the inspiration of the Holy Spirit, and
then through the Spirit also He began to lead the Church
into a recognition of these books as her canonical New
Testament Scripture.

During the second century, however, Satan endeavored
to confuse the Church by raising up deceitful men who
wrote pseudonymous works, falsely claiming to be
apostolic. These satanic devices hindered and delayed the
Church's recognition of the true New Testament canon but
could not prevent it. Soon after the beginning of the fifth
century the opposition of the devil was completely overcome. Under the leading of the Holy Spirit the Church was
guided to receive only the twenty-seven New Testament
books as canonical and to reject all others.

Dean Burgon believed that the history of the New Testament text was similar to the history of the New Testament
canon, and all orthodox Christians will do well to agree
with him in this, for study of the New Testament manuscripts bears him out. In other words, during the early
Christian centuries Satan directed his assault not only on
the New Testament canon but also on the New Testament
text. No sooner had the New Testament books been given
to the Church through the inspiration of the Holy Spirit
but the Spirit of Darkness began his endeavors to corrupt
their texts and render them useless. But in these efforts
also the evil one failed to attain his objective. In regard to

the New Testament text as well as in regard to the New Testament canon God bestowed on His Church sufficient grace to enable her to overcome all the wiles of the devil. Just as God guided the Church to reject, after a period of doubt and conflict, all noncanonical writings and to receive only the true canonical New Testament books, so God guided the Church during this same period to reject false readings and to receive into common usage the true New Testament text.

For an orthodox Christian, Burgon's view is the only reasonable one. If we believe that God gave the Church guidance in regard to the New Testament books, then surely it is logical to believe that God gave the Church similar guidance in regard to the text which these books contained. Surely it is very inconsistent to believe that God guided the Church in regard to the New Testament *canon* but gave her no guidance in regard to the New Testament *text.* But this seems to be just what many modern Christians do believe. They believe that all during the medieval period and throughout the Reformation and post-Reformation era the true New Testament text was lost and that it was not regained until the middle of the nineteenth century, when Tischendorf discovered it in the Sinaitic manuscript Aleph and when Westcott and Hort found it in the Vatican manuscript B.

Such inconsistency, however, is bound to lead to a skepticism which deprives the New Testament text of all authority. If we must believe that the true New Testament text was lost for fifteen hundred years, how can we be certain that it has now been found? What guarantee have we that either B or Aleph contain the true text? How can we be sure that Harris (1908), Conybeare (1910), Lake (1941), and other radical critics are not correct in their suspicions that the true New Testament text has been lost beyond possibility of recovery?

According to Burgon, the fundamental mistake of contemporary New Testament textual critics was that they ignored the unique character of the New Testament text. They would not recognize that they were dealing with a Book that was different from all other books—in short, with a Divinely inspired and providentially preserved Book.

That which distinguishes sacred science from every

other science which can be named is that it is Divine; furthermore, it has to do with a Book which is inspired and not regarded on a level with those books of the East that are held by their votaries to be sacred. It is chiefly from inattention to this circumstance that misconception prevails in that department of sacred science known as "textual criticism." Aware that the New Testament is *like no other book* in its origin, its contents, and its history, many critics of the present day nevertheless permit themselves to reason concerning its text, as if they entertained no suspicion that the words and sentences of which it is composed were destined to experience an extraordinary fate also. They make no allowance for the fact that influences of an entirely different kind from those with which profane literature is acquainted have made themselves felt in this department, and therefore that even those principles of textual criticism which in the case of profane authors are regarded as fundamental are often out of place here.

We see the fundamental difference between Burgon's approach to the problem of the New Testament text and that adopted by his contemporaries, especially Westcott and Hort. In matters of textual criticism, at least, these latter scholars followed a naturalistic method. They took particular pride in handling the text of the New Testament just as they would the text of any other ancient book. "For ourselves," Hort declared, "we dare not introduce considerations which could not reasonably be applied to other ancient texts, supposing them to have documentary attestation of equal amount, variety, and antiquity."

Burgon, on the other hand, followed a consistently Christian method of New Testament textual criticism. He believed that the New Testament had been Divinely inspired and providentially preserved; and when he came to the study of the New Testament text, he did not for one instant lay this faith aside. On the contrary, he regarded the Divine inspiration and providential preservation of the New Testament as two fundamental facts which must be taken into account in the interpretation of the details of New Testament textual criticism, two basic verities which make the textual criticism of the New Testament different from the textual criticism of any other book.

The evidence which has accumulated since Burgon's day is amply sufficient to justify the view held by him and by all consistently orthodox Christians—namely, that it was through the Church that Christ has fulfilled His promise always to preserve the true New Testament text, and that therefore the Byzantine text found in the vast majority of the Greek New Testament manuscripts is that true text. To reject this view is to act unreasonably. It is to fly in the face of the facts.

In like manner, those who reject this orthodox view of the New Testament text have rejected not merely the facts but also the promise of Christ always to preserve the true New Testament text and the doctrines of the Divine inspiration and providential preservation of Scripture implied in this promise.

Has Christ kept this promise or has He not? If we believe this promise, then we must do as Burgon and other orthodox Christians have done. Like Burgon, we must allow this promise to guide us in our dealings with the New Testament text. We must interpret all the data of New Testament textual criticism in the light of this promise.

It is just here, however, that many Christians are fatally inconsistent. They say they believe in Christ's promise to preserve the true New Testament text, but in practice they ignore this promise and treat the text of the New Testament exactly like that of an ordinary book concerning which no such promise has been made. Thus they are guilty of a basic unfaithfulness. In their efforts to be pleasing to naturalistic critics they themselves have lapsed into unbelief. They have undermined their own faith and deprived themselves of all ground for confidence in the infallibility of the Bible. For if the New Testament is just an ordinary book, then the trustworthiness of its text is, at best, only a probability, never a certainty.

Dean Burgon has a message for these waverers and for all who desire to attain to a firmer faith. In his controversy with the revisionists of 1881 Burgon stood forth as the uncompromising champion of the King James (Authorized) Version. "As a companion in the study and for private edification: as a book of reference for critical purposes, especially in respect of difficult and controverted passages—we hold that a revised edition of the Authorized Version of our English Bible (if executed with consummate ability and learning) would at any time be a work of inestimable value. The method of such a performance, whether by marginal notes or in some other way, we forbear to determine. But certainly only as a handmaid is it to be desired. As something intended to supersede our present English Bible, we are thoroughly convinced that the project of rival Translation is not to be entertained for a moment. For ourselves we deprecate it entirely."

Burgon's main purpose, however, was to defend the Byzantine (Traditional) text of the Greek New Testament on which the King James Version is based. He was removed from earth, it is true, before he could complete his grand design; but even before his death he had in great measure accomplished his purpose. Christians who desire to study the problems of the New Testament text should make every effort to procure Dean Burgon's works for their own possession. From him they will learn what it is to take first the standpoint of faith and then to deal faithfully and conscientiously with all the pertinent facts.

THE LAST TWELVE VERSES
OF THE GOSPEL
ACCORDING TO ST. MARK

John W. Burgon

Condensed by
David Otis Fuller, D.D.

THE LAST TWELVE VERSES
OF THE GOSPEL ACCORDING TO ST. MARK

Letter of Dedication

To
Sir Roundell Palmer, Q.C., M.P., &c.

Dear Sir Roundell,

I do myself the honor of inscribing this volume to you. Permit me to explain the reason why.

It is not merely that I may give expression to a sentiment of private friendship which dates back from the pleasant time when I was curate to your father—whose memory I never recall without love and veneration; nor even in order to afford myself the opportunity of testifying how much I honor you for the noble example of conscientious uprightness and integrity which you set us on a recent public occasion. It is for no such reason that I dedicate to you this vindication of the last twelve verses of the Gospel According to St. Mark.

It is because I desire to submit the argument contained in the ensuing pages to a practiced judicial intellect of the loftiest stamp. Recent editors of the New Testament insist that these "last twelve verses" are not genuine. The critics, almost to a man, avow themselves of the same opinion. Popular prejudice has been for a long time past warmly enlisted on the same side. I am as convinced as I am of my life, that the reverse is the truth. It is not even with me as it is with certain learned friends of mine, who, admitting the adversary's premises, content themselves with denying the validity of his inference. However true it may be—and it is true—that from those premises the proposed conclusion does not follow, I yet venture to deny the correctness of those premises altogether. I insist, on the contrary, that the evidence relied on is untrustworthy—untrustworthy in every particular.

How, in the meantime, can such a one as I am hope to persuade the world that it is as I say, while the most illustrious Biblical critics at home and abroad are agreed, and against me? Clearly, the first thing to be done is to secure for myself a full and patient hearing. With this view, I have written a book. But next, instead of waiting for the slow verdict of public opinion (which yet, I know, must come after many days), I desiderate for the evidence I have collected a competent and an impartial judge. And that is why I dedicate my book to you. If I can but get this case fairly tried, I have no doubt whatever about the result.

Whether you are able to find time to read these pages or not, it shall content me to have shown in this manner the confidence with which I advocate my cause; the kind of test to which I propose to bring my reasonings. If I may be allowed to say so, St. Mark's last twelve verses shall no longer remain a subject of dispute among men. I am able to prove that this portion of the Gospel has been declared to be spurious on wholly mistaken grounds, and this ought in fairness to close the discussion. But I claim to have done more. I claim to have shown, from considerations which have been hitherto overlooked, that its genuineness must needs be reckoned among the things that are absolutely certain.

I am, with sincere regard and respect,
Dear Sir Roundell,
Very faithfully yours,
JOHN W. BURGON

Oriel,
July, 1871

Preface

This volume is my contribution toward the better understanding of a subject which is destined, when it will have grown into a science, to vindicate for itself a mighty province, and to enjoy paramount attention. I allude to the textual criticism of the New Testament Scriptures.

That this study is still in its infancy, all may see. The very principles on which it is based are as yet only imperfectly understood. The reason is obvious. It is because the very foundations have not yet been laid (except to a wholly inadequate extent) on which the future superstructure is to rise. A careful collation of every extant codex (executed after the manner of the Rev. F. H. Scrivener's labors in this department) is the first indispensable preliminary to any real progress. Another is a revised text, not to say a more exact knowledge, of the oldest versions.

Scarcely of inferior importance would be critically correct editions of the Fathers of the Church; and these must by all means be furnished with far completer indices of texts than have ever yet been attempted. There is not a single Father to be named whose works have been hitherto furnished with even a tolerably complete index of the places in which he either quotes, or else clearly refers to, the text of the New Testament: while scarcely a tithe of the known MSS of the Gospels have as yet been satisfactorily collated. Strange to relate, we are to this hour without so much as a satisfactory catalog of the copies which are known to be extant.

But when all this has been done (and the science deserves, and requires, a little more public encouragement than has hitherto been bestowed on the arduous and—let me not be ashamed to add the word—unremunerative labor of textual criticism), it will be discovered that the popular and the prevailing theory is a mistaken one. The plausible hypothesis on which recent recensions of the text have been for the most part conducted will be seen to be no longer tenable. The latest decisions will in consequence be generally reversed.

I am not of course losing sight of what has been already achieved in this department of sacred learning. While our knowledge of the uncial MSS has been rendered tolerably exact and complete, an excellent beginning has been made (chiefly by the Rev. F. H. Scrivener, the most judicious living master of textual criticism) in acquainting us with the contents of about seventy of the cursive MSS of the New Testament. And though it is impossible to deny that the published texts of Doctors Tischendorf and Tregelles as texts are wholly inadmissible, yet is it equally certain that by the conscientious diligence with which those distinguished scholars have respectively labored, they have erected monuments of their learning and ability which will endure forever. Their editions of the New Testament will not be superseded by any new discoveries, by any future advances in the science of textual criticism. The MSS which they have edited will remain among the most precious materials for future study. All honor to them! If in the warmth of controversy I shall appear to have spoken of them sometimes without becoming deference, let me here once for all confess that I am to blame, and express my regret. When they have publicly begged St. Mark's pardon for the grievous wrong they have done him, I will very humbly beg their pardon also.

John Burgon

The Case of the Last Twelve Verses of St. Mark's Gospel Stated

It has lately become the fashion to speak of the last twelve verses of the Gospel According to St. Mark as if it were an ascertained fact that those verses constitute no integral part of the Gospel. It seems to be generally supposed (1) that the evidence of MSS is altogether fatal to their claims; (2) that "the early Fathers" witness plainly against their genuineness; and (3) that, from considerations of "internal evidence" they must certainly be given up. It will be my endeavor in the ensuing pages to show, on the contrary, that manuscript evidence is so overwhelmingly in their favor that no room is left for doubt or suspicion; that there is not so much as one of the Fathers, early or late, who gives it as his opinion that these verses are spurious; and, that the argument derived from internal considerations proves on inquiry to be baseless and as unsubstantial as a dream.

But I hope that I shall succeed in doing more. It will be my endeavor to show not only that there really is no reason whatever for calling in question the genuineness of this portion of Holy Writ, but also that there exist sufficient reasons for feeling confident that it must needs be genuine. This is clearly as much as it is possible for me to achieve. But when this has been done, I venture to hope that the verses in dispute will for the future be allowed to retain their place in the second Gospel unmolested.

It will of course be asked, And yet, if all this be so, how does it happen that both in very ancient, and also in very modern times, this proposal to suppress twelve verses of the Gospel has enjoyed a certain amount of popularity? At the two different periods (I answer), for widely different reasons.

In the ancient days, when it was the universal belief of Christendom that the Word of God must needs be consistent with itself in every part, and prove in every part (like its Divine Author) perfectly "faithful and true," the difficulty (which has deemed all but insuperable) of bringing certain statements in St. Mark's last twelve verses into harmony with certain statements of the other Evangelists, is discovered to have troubled Divines exceedingly. "In fact," says Mr. Scrivener, "it brought suspicion upon these verses, and caused their omission in some copies seen by Eusebius."

That the maiming process is indeed attributable to this cause and came about in this desire to provide an escape from a serious critical difficulty did not actually occasion that copies of St. Mark's Gospel were mutilated, it certainly was the reason why, in very early times, such mutilated copies were viewed without displeasure by some, and appealed to with complacency by others.

But times are changed. We have recently been assured on high authority that the Church has reversed her ancient convictions in this respect: that now, "most sound theologians have no dread whatever of acknowledging minute points of disagreement (i.e., minute errors) in the fourfold narrative even of the life of the Redeemer."

There has arisen in these last days a singular impatience of dogmatic truth (especially dogma of an unpalatable kind), which has even rendered popular the pretext afforded by these same mutilated copies for the grave resuscitation of doubts, never as it would seem seriously entertained by any of the ancients; and which, at all events for thirteen hundred years and upward, have deservedly sunk into oblivion.

Modern prejudice, then—added to a singularly exaggerated estimate of the critical importance of the testimony of our two oldest codices (another of the "discoveries of later times," concerning which I shall have

more to say by and by)—must explain why the opinion is
even popular that the last twelve verses of St. Mark are a
spurious appendix to his Gospel.

Not that biblical critics would have us believe that the
Evangelist left off at verse 8, intending that the words,
"neither said they anything to any man, for they were
afraid," should be the conclusion of his Gospel. "No one
can imagine," writes Griesbach, "that Mark cut short the
thread of his narrative at that place."

It is on all hands eagerly admitted that so abrupt a
termination must be held to mark an incomplete or else an
uncompleted work. How, then, in the original autograph
of the Evangelist, is it supposed that the narrative proceeded? This is what no one has even ventured so much as
to conjecture. It is assumed, however, that the original
termination of the Gospel, whatever it may have been, has
perished. We appeal, of course, to its actual termination:
and, of what nature then (we ask) is the supposed necessity for regarding the last twelve verses of St. Mark's
Gospel as a spurious substitute for what the Evangelist
originally wrote? What, in other words, has been the
history of these modern doubts; and by what steps have
they established themselves in books and won the public
ear?

To explain this will be the object of the ensuing
chapters.

The Hostile Verdict of Biblical Critics
Shown to Be Quite of Recent Date

It is only since the appearance of Griesbach's second
edition (1796-1806) that critics of the New Testament
have permitted themselves to handle the last twleve verses
of St. Mark's Gospel with disrespect. Previous critical editions of the New Testament are free from this reproach.
"There is no reason for doubting the genuineness of this
portion of Scripture," wrote Mill in 1707, after a review of
the evidence (as far as he was acquainted with it) for and
against. Twenty-seven years later Bengel's edition of the
New Testament appeared (1734); and Wetstein, at the end
of another seventeen years (1751-52), followed in the
same field. Both editors, after rehearsing the adverse testimony *in extenso,* left the passage in undisputed possession
of its place.

Alter in 1786-87 and Birch in 1788 (suspicious as the latter evidently was of its genuineness) followed their predecessors' example. But Matthaei (who also brought his labors to a close in the year 1788) was not content to give a silent suffrage. He had been for upward of fourteen years a laborious collator of Greek MSS of the New Testament, and was so convinced of the insufficiency of the arguments which had been brought against these twelve verses of St. Mark, that with no ordinary warmth, no common acuteness, he insisted on their genuineness.

"With Griesbach," remarks Dr. Tregelles, "texts which may be called really critical begin"; and Griesbach is the first to insist that the concluding verses of St. Mark are spurious. That he did not suppose the second Gospel to have always ended at verse 8, we have seen already. He was of the opinion, however, that "at some very remote period, the original ending of the Gospel perished—disappeared perhaps from the Evangelist's own copy—and that the present ending was by someone substituted in its place."

It should be perhaps stated in passing that Griesbach was driven into this curious maze of unsupported conjecture by the exigencies of his "Recension Theory," which, inasmuch as it has been long since exploded, need not now occupy us. But it is worth observing that the argument already exhibited (such as it is) breaks down under the weight of the very first fact which its learned author is obliged to lay upon it. Codex B—the solitary manuscript witness for omitting the clause in question (for Codex Aleph had not yet been discovered)—had been already claimed by Griesbach as a chief exponent of his so-called Alexandrine Recension. But then, on the critic's own hypothesis (as we have seen already) Codex B ought, on the contrary, to have contained it.

How was that inconvenient fact to be got over? Griesbach quietly remarks in a footnote that Codex B "has affinity with Eastern family of MSS." The misfortune of being saddled with a worthless theory was surely never more apparent. By the time we have reached this point in the investigation we are reminded of nothing so much as of the weary traveler who, having patiently pursued an ignis fatuus through half the night, beholds it at last to vanish—but not until it has conducted him up to his chin in the mire.

Neither Hug, nor Scholz his pupil—who in 1808 and 1830 respectively followed Griesbach with modifications of his recension theory—concurred in the unfavorable sentence which their illustrious predecessor had passed on the concluding portion of St. Mark's Gospel. The latter even eagerly vindicated its genuineness.

But with Lachmann—whose unsatisfactory text of the Gospels appeared in 1842—originated a new principle of textual revision; namely, paying exclusive and absolute deference to the testimony of a few arbitrarily selected ancient documents, no regard being paid to others of the same or of yet higher antiquity. This is not the right place for discussing this plausible and certainly most convenient scheme of textual revision. That it leads to conclusions little short of irrational is certain. I notice it only because it supplies the clue to the result which, as far as St. Mark 16:9-20 is concerned, has been since arrived at by Dr. Tischendorf, Dr. Tregelles, and Dean Alford—the three latest critics who have formally undertaken to reconstruct the sacred text.

They agree in assuring their readers that the genuine Gospel of St. Mark extends no further than chapter 16, verse 8; in other words, that all that follows the words *ephobounto gar* is an unauthorized addition by some later hand; "a fragment"—distinguishable from the rest of the Gospel not less by internal evidence than by external testimony. This verdict becomes the more important because it proceeds from men of undoubted earnestness and high ability, who cannot be suspected of being either unacquainted with the evidence on which the point in dispute rests nor inexperienced in the art of weighing such evidence.

Moreover, their verdict has been independently reached, is unanimous, is unhesitating, has been eagerly proclaimed by all three on many different occasions as well as in many different places, and may be said to be at present in all but undisputed possession of the field. The first named editor enjoys a vast reputation and has been generously styled by Mr. Scrivener as "the first Biblical Critic in Europe." The other two have produced textbooks which are deservedly held in high esteem and are in the hands of every student. The views of such men will undoubtedly color the convictions of the next generation of English churchmen.

It becomes absolutely necessary, therefore, to examine with the utmost care the grounds of their verdict, the direct result of which is to present us with a mutilated Gospel. If they are right, there is no help for it but that the convictions of eighteen centuries in this respect must be surrendered. But if Tischendorf and Tregelles are wrong in this particular, it follows of necessity that doubt is thrown over the whole of their critical method. The case is a crucial one. Every page of theirs incurs suspicion if their deliberate verdict in this instance will prove to be mistaken.

Tischendorf disposes of the whole question in a single sentence: "That these verses were not written by Mark admits of satisfactory proof." He then recites in detail the adverse external testimony which his predecessors had accumulated, remarking that it is abundantly confirmed by internal evidence. Of this he supplies a solitary sample, but declares that the whole passage is "abhorrent" to St. Mark's manner. "The facts of the case being such," and with this he dismisses the subject, "a healthy piety reclaims against the endeavors of those who are for palming off as Mark's what the Evangelist is so plainly shown to have known nothing at all about."

A mass of laborious annotation which comes surging in at the close of verse 8, and fills two of Tischendorf's pages, has the effect of entirely divorcing the twelve verses in question from the inspired text of the Evangelist. On the other hand, the evidence in favor of the place is dispatched in less than twelve lines. What can be the reason that an editor of the New Testament parades elaborately every particular of the evidence (such as it is) against the genuineness of a considerable portion of the Gospel, and yet makes summary work with the evidence in its favor? That Tischendorf has at least entirely made up his mind on the matter in hand is plain. Elsewhere he speaks of the author of these verses as "Pseudo Marcus."

Dr. Tregelles has expressed himself most fully on this subject in his "Account of the Printed Text of the Greek New Testament" (1854). The respected author undertakes to show "that the early testimony that St. Mark did not write these verses is confirmed by existing monuments." Accordingly, he announces as the result of the propositions which he thinks he has established, "The book of

Mark itself extends no further than *ephobounto gar.* "

He is the only critic I have met with to whom it does not seem incredible that St. Mark did actually conclude his Gospel in this abrupt way: observing that "perhaps we do not know enough of the circumstances of St. Mark when he wrote his Gospel to say whether he did or did not leave it with a complete termination."

In this modest suggestion at least Dr. Tregelles is unassailable, since we know absolutely nothing whatever about "the circumstances of St. Mark [or of any other Evangelist] when he wrote his Gospel . . . neither indeed are we quite sure who St. Mark was."

But when he goes on to declare, notwithstanding, "that the remaining twelve verses, by whomsoever written, have a full claim to be received as an authentic part of the second Gospel" and complains that "there is in some minds a kind of timidity with regard to Holy Scripture, as if all our notions of its authority depended on our knowing who was the writer of each particular portion; instead of simply seeing and owning that it was given forth from God, and that it is as much His as were the commandments of the law written by His own finger on the tables of stone," the learned writer betrays a misapprehension of the question at issue, which we are least of all prepared to encounter in such a quarter.

We admire his piety but it is at the expense of his critical sagacity. For the question is not at all one of authorship but only one of genuineness. Have the codices been mutilated which do not contain these verses? If they have, then these verses must be held to be genuine. But on the contrary, have the codices been supplemented which contain them? Then these verses are certainly spurious.

There is not help for it but they must either be held to be an integral part of the Gospel, and therefore, in default of any proof to the contrary, as certainly by St. Mark as any other twelve verses which can be named; or else an unauthorized addition to it. If they belong to the post-apostolic age it is idle to insist on their inspiration and to claim that this "authentic anonymous addition to what Mark himself wrote down" is as much the work of God "as were the Ten Commandments written by His own finger on the tables of stone."

On the other hand, if they "ought as much to be

received as part of our second Gospel as the last chapter of
Deuteronomy (unknown as the writer is) is received as the
right and proper conclusion of the book of Moses," it is
difficult to understand why the learned editor should
think himself at liberty to sever them from their context
and introduce the subscription *KATA MAPKON* after
verse 8.

In short, "how persons who believe that these verses did
not form a part of the original Gospel of Mark, but were
added afterwards, can say that they have a good claim to
be received as an authentic or genuine part of the second
Gospel, that is, a portion of canonical Scripture, passes
comprehension." It passes even Dr. Davidson's comprehension (for the foregoing words are his); and Dr.
Davidson, as some of us are aware, is not a man to stick at
trifles.

Dean Alford went a little further than any of his
predecessors. He says that this passage "was placed as a
completion of the Gospel soon after the Apostolic
period—the Gospel itself having been, for some reason
unknown to us, left incomplete."

"The most probable supposition," he adds, "is, that the
last leaf of the original Gospel was torn away." The
internal evidence (declares the same learned writer)
"preponderates vastly against the authorship of Mark" or
(as he elsewhere expresses it) against "its genuineness as a
work of the Evangelist." Accordingly, in his Prolegomena
he describes it as "the remarkable fragment at the end of
the Gospel."

After this, we are the less astonished to find that he
closes the second Gospel at verse 8, introduces the subscription there, and encloses the twelve verses which
follow within heavy brackets. Thus, whereas from the days
of our illustrious countryman Mill (1707) the editors of
the New Testament have either been silent on the subject
or else have whispered only that this section of the Gospel
is to be received with less of confidence than the rest, it
has been reserved for the present century to convert the
ancient suspicions into actual charges. The latest to enter
the field have been the first to execute Griesbach's adverse
sentence pronounced fifty years ago and to load the
blessed Evangelist with bonds.

It might have been foreseen that when critics so conspicuous permit themselves thus to handle the precious deposit, others would take courage to hurl their thunderbolts in the same direction with the less concern. "It is probable," says Archbishop Thomson in the Bible dictionary, "that this section is from a different hand, and was annexed to the Gospels soon after the times of the apostles." The Rev. T. S. Green an able scholar, never to be mentioned without respect, considers that "the hypothesis of very early interpolation satisfies the body of facts in evidence, [which] point unmistakably in the direction of a spurious origin."

"In respect of Mark's Gospel," writes Professor Norton in a recent work on the genuineness of the Gospels, "there is ground for believing that the last twelve verses were not written by the Evangelist but were added by some other writer to supply a short conclusion to the work, which some cause had prevented the author from completing." Professor Westcott—who, jointly with the Rev. F.J.A. Hort, announces a revised text—assures us that "the original text, from whatever cause it may have happened, terminated abruptly after the account of the angelic vision." The rest "was added at another time, and probably by another hand. . . . It is in vain to speculate on the causes of this abrupt close. . . . The remaining verses cannot be regarded as part of the original narrative of St. Mark."

Meyer insists that this is an "apocryphal fragment" and reproduces all the arguments—external and internal—which have ever been arrayed against it, without a particle of misgiving. The "note" with which he takes leave of the subject is even insolent. A comparison (he says) of these "fragments" (vv. 9-18, 19) with the parallel places in the other Gospels and in the Acts, shows how vacillating and various were the apostolical traditions concerning the appearances of our Lord after His resurrection, and concerning His ascension. ("Hast thou killed, and also taken possession?")

Such, then, is the hostile verdict concerning these last twelve verses which I venture to dispute, and which I trust I shall live to see reversed. The writers above cited (1) will be found to rely on the external evidence of certain ancient MSS and (2) on scholia which state "that the more ancient and accurate copies terminated the Gospel at verse

8"; (3) assure us that this is confirmed by a formidable array of patristic authorities; and that (4) internal proof is not to be wanting. Certain incoherences and inaccuracies are pointed out. In fine, "the phraseology and style of the section" are declared to be "unfavorable to its authenticity," not a few of the words and expressions being "foreign to the diction of Mark." I propose to show that all these confident and imposing statements are to a great extent either mistakes or exaggerations, and that the slender residuum of fact is about as powerless to achieve the purpose of the critics as were the seven green withes of the Philistines to bind Samson.

In order to exhibit successfully what I have to offer on this subject, I find it necessary to begin (in the next chapter) at the very beginning. I think it right, however, in this place to premise a few plain considerations which will be of use to us throughout all our subsequent inquiry, and which indeed we shall never be able to afford to lose sight of for long.

The question at issue being simply this, whether it is reasonable to suspect that the last twelve verses of St. Mark are a spurious accretion and unauthorized supplement to his Gospel or not, the whole of our business clearly resolves itself into an examination of what has been urged in proof that the former alternative is the correct one.

Our opponents maintain that these verses did not form part of the original autograph of the Evangelist. But it is a known rule in the law of evidence that the burden of proof lies on the party who asserts the affirmative of the issue. We have therefore to ascertain in the present instance what the supposed proof is exactly worth, remembering always that in this subject matter a high degree of probability is the only kind of proof which is attainable. When, for example, it is contended that the famous words in St. John's First Epistle (I John 5:7, 8) are not to be regarded as genuine, the fact that they are away from almost every known codex is accepted as a proof that they were also away from the autograph of the Evangelist. On far less weighty evidence, in fact, we are at all times prepared to yield the hearty assent of our understanding in this department of sacred science.

And yet it will be found that evidence of overwhelming

weight, if not of an entirely different kind, is required in the present instance.

The case is altogether different, as all must see, when it is proposed to get rid of the twelve verses which for seventeen hundred years and upward have formed the conclusion of St. Mark's Gospel, no alternative conclusion being proposed to our acceptance. For let it be only observed what this proposal practically amounts to and means.

And, first, it does not mean that St. Mark himself, with design, brought his Gospel to a close at the words *ephobounto gar*. That supposition would in fact be irrational. It does not mean, I say, that by simply leaving out those last twelve verses we shall be restoring the second Gospel to its original integrity. And this it is which makes the present a different case from every other and necessitates a fuller, if not a different, kind of proof.

What then? It means that although an abrupt and impossible termination would confessedly be the result of omitting verses 9-20, no nearer approximation to the original autograph of the Evangelist is at present attainable. Whether St. Mark was interrupted before he could finish his Gospel (as Dr. Tregelles and Professor Norton suggest—in which case it will have been published by its author in an unfinished state) or whether "the last leaf was torn away" before a single copy of the original could be procured (a view which is found to have recommended itself to Griesbach—in which case it will have once had a different termination from at present; which termination however, by the hypothesis, has since been irrecoverably lost; and to one of these two wild hypotheses the critics are logically reduced), this we are not certainly told. The critics are only agreed in assuming that St. Mark's Gospel was at first without the verses which at present conclude it.

But this assumption (that a work which has been held to be a complete work for seventeen centuries and upward was originally incomplete) of course requires proof. The forgoing improbable theories, based on a gratuitous assumption, are confronted *in limine* with a formidable obstacle which must be absolutely got rid of before they can be thought entitled to a serious hearing.

It is a familiar and a fatal circumstance that the Gospel

of St. Mark has been furnished with its present termination
ever since the second century of the Christian era. In
default, therefore, of distinct historical evidence or
definite documentary proof that at some earlier period it
terminated abruptly, nothing short of the utter unfitness
of the verses which at present conclude St. Mark's Gospel
to be regarded as the work of the Evangelist, would
warrant us in assuming that they are the spurious accretion
of the postapostolic age and as such, at the end of eighteen
centuries, to be deliberately rejected.

We must absolutely be furnished, I say, with internal
evidence of the most unequivocal character or else with
external testimony of a direct and definite kind, if we are
to admit that the actual conclusion of St. Mark's Gospel is
an unauthorized substitute for something quite different
that has been lost.

I can only imagine one other thing which could induce
us to entertain such an opinion, and that would be the
general consent of MSS, Fathers, and versions in leaving
these verses out. Else it is evident that we are logically
forced to adopt the far easier supposition that (not St.
Mark, but) some copyist of the third century left a copy of
St. Mark's Gospel unfinished, which unfinished copy
became the fontal source of the mutilated copies that have
come down to our own times.

I have thought it right to explain the matter thus fully
at the outset, not in order to prejudge the question (for
that could answer no good purpose) but only in order that
the reader may have clearly set before him the real nature
of the issue. "Is it reasonable to suspect that the concluding verses of St. Mark are a spurious accretion and
unauthorized supplement to his Gospel, or not?" That is
the question which we have to consider—the one question.
And while I proceed to pass under careful review all the
evidence on this subject with which I am acquainted, I
shall be again and again obliged to direct the attention of
my reader to its bearing on the real point at issue.

In other words, we shall have again and again to ask
ourselves, How far is it rendered probable by each fresh
article of evidence that St. Mark's Gospel, when it left the
hands of its inspired author, was an unfinished work, the
last chapter ending abruptly at verse 8?

I will only point out, before passing on, that the course

which has been adopted toward St. Mark 16:9-20 by the latest editors of the New Testament is simply illogical. Either they regard these verses as possibly genuine or else as certainly spurious. If they entertain (as they say they do) a decided opinion that they are not genuine, they ought (if they would be consistent) to banish them from the text. Conversely, since they do not banish them from the text, they have no right to pass a fatal sentence on them, to designate their author as "Pseudo Marcus," or to handle them in contemptuous fashion.

The plain truth is, these learned men are better than their theory, the worthlessness of which they are made to feel in the present most conspicuous instance. It reduces them to perplexity. It has landed them in inconsistency and error. They will find it necessary in the end to reverse their convictions. They cannot too speedily reconsider their verdict and retrace their steps.

The Early Fathers Appealed to, and Observed to Bear Favorable Witness

It is well known that for determining the text of the New Testament we are dependent on three chief sources of information: manuscripts, versions, and Fathers. And it is even self-evident that the most ancient MSS, the earliest versions, and the oldest of the Fathers will probably be in every instance the most trustworthy witnesses.

On the other hand, it cannot be too plainly pointed out that when, instead of certifying ourselves of the actual words employed by an Evangelist, their precise form and exact sequence, our object is only to ascertain whether a considerable passage of Scripture is genuine or not; is to be rejected or retained; was known or was not known in the earliest ages of the Church; then, instead of supplying the least important evidence, Fathers become by far the most valuable witnesses of all. This entire subject may be conveniently illustrated by an appeal to the problem before us.

Of course, if we possessed copies of the Gospels coeval with their authors, nothing could compete with such evidence. But then unhappily nothing of the kind is the case. The facts admit of being stated within the compass of a few lines. We have one codex (the Vatican, B), which is thought to belong to the first half of the fourth century, and another, the newly discovered Codex Sinaiticus (at St. Petersburg, Aleph), which is certainly not quite so old, perhaps by fifty years.

Next come two famous codices: the Alexandrine (in the British Museum, A) and the Codex Ephraemi (in the Paris Library, C), which are probably from fifty to one hundred years more recent still. The Codex Bezae (at Cambridge, D) is considered by competent judges to be the depository of a recension of the text as ancient as any of the others. Our primitive manuscript witnesses, therefore, are but five in number at the utmost. And of these it has never been pretended that the oldest is to be referred to an earlier date than the beginning of the fourth century, while it is thought by competent judges that the last named may very possibly have been written quite late in the sixth.

Are we then reduced to this fourfold (or at most five-fold) evidence concerning the text of the Gospels—on evidence of not quite certain date, and yet (as we all believe) not reaching further back than to the fourth century of our era? Certainly not. Here, Fathers come to our aid. There are perhaps as many as a hundred ecclesiastical writers older than the oldest extant codex of the New Testament, while between A.D. 300 and A.D. 600 (within which limits our five oldest MSS may be considered certainly to fall) there exist about two hundred more Fathers.

True, many of these have left wondrous little behind them and the quotations from Holy Scripture of the greater part may justly be described as rare and unsatisfactory. But what then? From the three hundred, make a liberal reduction; a hundred writers will remain who frequently quote the New Testament, and who, when they do quote it, are probably as trustworthy witnesses to the truth of Scripture as either Codex Aleph or Codex B.

We have indeed heard a great deal too much of the precariousness of this class of evidence and not nearly enough of the gross inaccuracies which disfigure the text of those two codices. It is quite surprising to discover to what an extent patristic quotations from the New Testament have evidently retained their exact original form.

For let it be only considered what is implied by a patristic appeal to the Gospel. It amounts to this: a conspicuous personage, probably a bishop of the Church—one,

therefore, whose history, date, place, are all more or less
matter of notoriety—gives us his written assurance that the
passage in question was found in that copy of the Gospels
which he was accustomed himself to employ: the uncial
codex (it has long since perished) which belonged to himself or the Church he served.

It is evident, in short, that any objection to quotations
from Scripture in the writings of the ancient Fathers can
only apply to the form of those quotations, not to their
substance. It is just as certain that a verse of Scripture was
actually read by the Father who unmistakably refers to it,
as if we had read it with him, even though the gravest
doubts may be entertained as to the *ipsissima verba* which
were found in his own particular copy. He may have
trusted to his memory; or copyists may have taken
liberties with his writings; or editors may have misrepresented what they found in the written copies.

The form of the quoted verse, I repeat, may have
suffered almost to any extent. The substance, on the contrary, inasmuch as it lay wholly beyond their province,
may be looked on as an indisputable fact.

Some such preliminary remarks (never out of place
when quotations from the Fathers are to be considered)
cannot well be withheld when the most venerable ecclesiastical writings are appealed to. The earliest of the Fathers
are observed to quote with singular license—to allude
rather than to quote. Strange to relate, those ancient men
seem scarcely to have been aware of the grave responsibility they incurred when they substituted expressions of
their own for the utterances of the Spirit. It is evidently
not so much that their memory is in fault as their judgment, in that they evidently hold themselves at liberty to
paraphrase, to recast, to reconstruct.

Ambrose, Archbishop of Milan (A.D. 374-397), freely
quotes this portion of the Gospel, citing verse 15 four
times; verses 16, 17, and 18, each three times; verse 20
once.

The testimony of Chrysostom (A.D. 400) has been all
but overlooked. In part of a homily claimed for him by his
Benedictine editors, he points out that St. Luke alone of
the Evangelists describes the ascension: St. Matthew and
St. John not speaking of it, St. Mark recording the event
only. Then he quotes verses 19, 20. "This," he adds, "is

the end of the Gospel. Mark makes no extended mention of the ascension." Elsewhere he has an unmistakable reference to St. Mark 16:9.

Jerome, on a point like this, is entitled to more attention than any other Father of the Church. Living at a very early period (for he was born in 331 and died in 420), endowed with extraordinary biblical learning, a man of excellent judgment, and a professed editor of the New Testament (for the execution of which task he enjoyed extraordinary facilities), his testimony is most weighty.

Not unaware am I that Jerome is commonly supposed to be a witness on the opposite side—concerning which mistake I shall have to speak largely in a subsequent chapter. But it ought to be enough to point out that we should not have met with these last twelve verses in the Vulgate, had Jerome held them to be spurious. He familiarly quotes the 9th verse in one place of his writings; in another place he makes the extraordinary statement that in certain of the copies (especially the Greek) was found after verse 14 the reply of the eleven apostles, when our Savior "upbraided them with their unbelief and hardness of heart, because they believed not them which had seen Him after He was risen." To discuss so weak and worthless a forgery—no trace of which is found in any MS in existence, and of which nothing whatever is known except what Jerome here tells us—would be to waste our time indeed. The fact remains, however, that Jerome, besides giving these last twelve verses a place in the Vulgate, quotes Mark 16:14, as well as verse 9, in the course of his writings.

It was to have been expected that Augustine would quote these verses, but he more than quotes them. He brings them forward again and again, discusses them as the work of St. Mark, and remarks that "in diebus Paschalibus," St. Mark's narrative of the resurrection was publicly read in the Church. All this is noteworthy. Augustine flourished A.D. 395-430.

Another very important testimony to the genuineness of the concluding part of St. Mark's Gospel is furnished by the unhesitating manner in which Nestorius the heresiarch quotes verse 20; and Cyril of Alexandria accepts his quotation, adding a few words of his own. Let it be borne in mind that this is tantamount to the discovery of two dated codices containing the last twelve verses of St. Mark—and that date anterior (it is impossible to say by how many years) to A.D. 430.

Hesychius of Jerusalem, by a singular oversight, has been reckoned among the impugners of these verses. He is on the contrary their eager advocate and champion. It seems to have escaped observation that toward the close of his "Homily on the Resurrection" (published in the works of Gregory of Nyssa, and erroneously ascribed to that Father) Hesychius appeals to the 19th verse and quotes it as St. Mark's at length. The date of Hesychius is uncertain; but he may, I suppose, be considered to belong to the sixth century. His evidence is discussed in a subsequent chapter.

The Early Versions Examined,
and Found to Yield Unfaltering Testimony
to the Genuineness of These Verses

It was declared at the outset that when we are seeking to establish in detail the text of the Gospels, the testimony of manuscripts is incomparably the most important of all. To early versions, the second place was assigned; to patristic citations, the third. But it was explained that whenever (as here) the only question to be decided is whether a considerable portion of Scripture be genuine or not, then, patristic references yield to no class of evidence in importance.

To which statement it must now be added that second only to the testimony of Fathers on such occasions is to be reckoned the evidence of the oldest of the versions. The reason is obvious. (a) We know for the most part the approximate date of the principal ancient versions of the New Testament; (b) each version is represented by at least one very ancient codex; (c) it may be safely assumed that translators were never dependent on a single copy of the original Greek when they executed their several translations. We now proceed to ascertain what evidence the oldest of the versions bear concerning the concluding verses of St. Mark's Gospel: and first of all for the Syriac.

"Literary history," says Mr. Scrivener, "can hardly afford a more powerful case than has been established for the identity of the version of the Syriac now called the 'Peshito' with that used by the Eastern Church long before the great schism had its beginning, in the native land of the blessed Gospel." The Peshito is referred by common consent to the second century of our era and is found to contain the verses in question.

This, however, is not all. Within the last thirty years, fragments of another very ancient Syriac translation of the Gospels (called from the name of its discoverer "The Curetonian Syriac") have come to light; and in this translation also the verses in question are found. This fragmentary codex is referred by Curetons to the middle of the fifth century.

At what earlier date the translation may have been executed—as well as how much older the original Greek copy may have been which this translator employed—can of course only be conjectured. But it is clear that we are listening to another truly primitive witness to the genuineness of the text now under consideration—a witness (like the last) vastly more ancient than either the Vatican Codex B or the Sinaitic Codex Aleph; more ancient, therefore, than any Greek copy of the Gospels in existence. We shall not be thought rash if we claim it for the third century.

The fact that Jerome, at the bidding of Pope Damasus (A.D. 382), was the author of that famous Latin version of the Scriptures called the Vulgate, is known to all. It seems scarcely possible to overestimate the critical importance of such a work, executed at such a time, under such auspices, and by a man of so much learning and sagacity as Jerome.

When it is considered that we are here presented with the results of a careful examination of the best Greek manuscripts to which a competent scholar had access in the middle of the fourth century (and Jerome assures us that he consulted several), we learn to survey with diminished complacency our own slender stores (if indeed any at all exist) of corresponding antiquity. It is needless to add that the Vulgate contains the disputed verses; from no copy of this version are they away. Now, in such a matter as this, Jerome's testimony is very weighty indeed.

The Vulgate, however, was but the revision of a much older translation, generally known as the Vetus Itala. This Old Latin, which is of African origin and of almost apostolic antiquity (supposedly of the second century), conspires with the Vulgate in the testimony which it bears to the genuineness of the end of St. Mark's Gospel: an emphatic witness that in the African province, from the earliest time, no doubt whatever was entertained concerning the genuineness of these last twelve verses.

The next place may well be given to the venerable version of the Gothic Bishop Ulphilas, A.D. 350. Himself a Cappadocian, Ulphilas probably derived his copies from Asia Minor. His version is said to have been exposed to certain corrupting influences, but the unequivocal evidence it bears to the last verses of St. Mark is at least unimpeachable and must be regarded as important in the highest degree. The oldest extant copy of the Gothic of Ulphilas is assigned to the fifth or early sixth century, and the verses in question are there also met with.

The ancient Egyptian versions call next for notice, their testimony being so exceedingly ancient and respectable. The Memphitic, or dialect of Lower Egypt (less properly called the "Coptic" version), which is assigned to the fourth or fifth century, contains St. Mark 16:9-20. Fragments of the Thebaic, or dialect of Upper Egypt (a distinct version and of considerably earlier date, less properly called the "Sahidic"), survive in MSS of very nearly the same antiquity; and one of these fragments happily contains the last verse of the Gospel According to St. Mark. The Thebaic version is referred to the third century.

In the fourth century (to which Codex B and Codex Aleph probably belong) five Greek writers, one Syriac, and two Latin Fathers—besides the Vulgate, Gothic and Memphitic Versions (eleven authorities in all)—testify to familiar acquaintance with this portion of St. Mark's Gospel.

In the third century (and by this time MS evidence has entirely forsaken us) we find Hippolytus, the Curetonian Syriac, and the Thebaic Version bearing plain testimony that at that early period, in at least three distinct provinces of primitive Christendom, no suspicion whatever attached to these verses. Lastly, in the second century, Irenaeus, the Peshito, and the Italic Version just as plainly attest that in Gaul, Mesopotamia, and the African province the same verses were unhesitatingly received within a century (more or less) of the date of the inspired autograph of the Evangelist himself.

Thus, we are in possession of the testimony of at least six independent witnesses, of a date considerably anterior to the earliest extant codex of the Gospels. They are all of the best class. They deliver themselves in the most unequivocal way. And their testimony to the genuineness of these verses is unfaltering.

It is clear that nothing short of direct adverse evidence of the weightiest kind can sensibly affect so formidable an array of independent authorities as this. What must the evidence be which will set it entirely aside and induce us to believe, with the most recent editors of the inspired text, that the last chapter of St. Mark's Gospel, as it came from the hands of its inspired author, ended abruptly at verse 8?

The grounds for assuming that his last twelve verses are spurious will be exhibited in the ensuing chapter.

The Alleged Hostile Witness
of Certain of the Early Fathers
Proved to Be an Imagination of the Critics

It would naturally follow to show that manuscript evidence confirms the evidence of the ancient Fathers and of the early versions of Scripture. But it will be more satisfactory that I should proceed to examine without more delay the testimony which (as it is alleged) is borne by a cloud of ancient Fathers against the last twelve verses of St. Mark. "The absence of this portion from some, from many, or from most copies of his Gospel, or that it was not written by St. Mark himself," says Dr. Tregelles, "is attested by Eusebius, Gregory of Nyssa, Victor of Antioch, Severus of Antioch, Jerome, and by later writers, especially Greeks."

The same Fathers are appealed to by Dr. Davidson, who adds to the list Euthymius; and by Tischendorf and Alford, who add the name of Hesychius of Jerusalem. They also refer to "many ancient scholia." "These verses," says Tischendorf, "are not recognized by the sections of Ammonius nor by the Canons of Eusebius; Epiphanius and Caesarius bear witness to the fact."

"In the Catenae on Mark," proceeds Davidson, "the section is not explained. Nor is there any trace of acquaintance with it on the part of Clement of Rome or Clement of Alexandria." This is a remark which others have made also; as if it were a surprising circumstance that Clement of Alexandria, who appears to have no reference to the last chapter of St. Matthew's Gospel, should be also without any reference to the last chapter of St. Mark's; as if, too, it were an extraordinary thing that Clement of Rome should have omitted to quote from the last chapter of St. Mark, seeing that the same Clement does not quote from St. Mark's Gospel at all. . . .

The alacrity displayed by learned writers in accumulating hostile evidence is certainly worthy of a better cause. Strange that their united industry should have been attended with such very unequal success when their object was to exhibit the evidence in favor of the present portion of Scripture.

Eusebius then, and Jerome; Gregory of Nyssa and Hesychius of Jerusalem; Severus of Antioch, Victor of Antioch, and Euthymius: do the accomplished critics just quoted—Doctors Tischendorf, Tregelles, and Davidson—really mean to tell us that "it is attested" by these seven Fathers that the concluding section of St. Mark's Gospel "was not written by St. Mark himself"? Why, there is not one of them who says so; while some of them say the direct reverse. But let us go on. It is, I suppose, because there are twelve verses to be demolished that the list is further eked out with the names of Ammonius, Epiphanius, and Caesarius, to say nothing of the anonymous authors of Catenae and "later writers, especially Greeks."

With respect to Eusebius the case is altogether different. What that learned Father has delivered concerning the conclusion of St. Mark's Gospel requires to be examined with attention, and must be set forth much more in detail. And yet, I will so far anticipate what is about to be offered, as to say at once that if any one supposes that Eusebius has anywhere plainly "stated that it is wanted in many MSS," he is mistaken. Eusebius nowhere says so. The reader's attention is invited to a plain tale.

It was not until 1825 that the world was presented by Cardinal Angelo Mai with a few fragmentary specimens of a lost work of Eusebius on the (so-called) *Inconsistencies in the Gospels,* from a MS in the Vatican. These, the learned cardinal republished more accurately in 1847, in his *Nova Patrum Bibliotheca,* and hither we are invariably referred by those who cite Eusebius as a witness against the genuineness of the concluding verses of the second

Gospel.

It is much to be regretted that we are still as little as ever in possession of the lost work of Eusebius. It appears to have consisted of three books or parts, the former two (addressed "To Stephanus") being discussions of difficulties at the beginning of the Gospel, the last ("To Marinus") relating to difficulties in its concluding chapters. The author's plan (as usual in such works) was, first, to set forth a difficulty in the form of a question, then straightway to propose a solution of it—which commonly assumes the form of a considerable dissertation. But we may reasonably doubt whether we are at present in possession of so much as a single entire specimen of these *Inquiries and Resolutions* exactly as it came from the pen of Eusebius.

That the work which Mai has brought to light is but a highly condensed exhibition of the original (and scarcely that) its very title shows; for it is headed, "An abridged selection from the *Inquiries and Resolutions* (of difficulties) in the Gospels by Eusebius." Only some of the original questions, therefore, are here noticed at all; and even these have been subjected to so severe a process of condensation and abridgment that in some instances amputation would probably be a more fitting description of what has taken place.

It has been urged that Eusebius cannot have recognized the verses in question as genuine, because a scholium purporting to be his has been cited by Matthaei from a Catena at Moscow in which he appears to assert that "according to Mark," our Savior "is not recorded to have appeared to His disciples after His resurrection"; whereas in St. Mark 16:14 it is plainly recorded that "afterwards he appeared unto the eleven as they sat at meat."

May I be permitted to declare that I am distrustful of the proposed inference, and shall continue to feel so, until I know something more about the scholium in question? Up to the time when this page is printed I have not succeeded in obtaining from Moscow the details I wish for, but they must be already on the way, and I propose to embody the result in a postscript which shall form the last page of the appendix to the present volume.

Are we then to suppose that there was no substratum of truth in the allegations to which Eusebius gives such prominence in the passage under discussion? By no means. The mutilated state of St. Mark's Gospel in the Vatican Codex (B) and especially in the Sinaitic Codex (Aleph) sufficiently establishes the contrary.

Let it be freely conceded (but in fact it has been freely conceded already) that there must have existed in the time of Eusebius many copies of St. Mark's Gospel which were without the twelve concluding verses. I do but insist that there is nothing whatever in that circumstance to lead us to entertain one serious doubt as to the genuineness of these verses. I am but concerned to maintain that there is nothing whatever in the evidence which has hitherto come before us—certainly not in the evidence of Eusebius—to induce us to believe that they are a spurious addition to St. Mark's Gospel.

We have next to consider what Jerome has delivered on this subject. So great a name must needs command attention in any question of textual criticism, and it is commonly pretended that Jerome pronounces emphatically against the genuineness of the last twelve verses of the Gospel According to St. Mark. A little attention to the actual testimony borne by this Father will, it is thought, suffice to exhibit it in a wholly unexpected light and induce us to form an entirely different estimate of its practical bearing on the present discussion.

It will be convenient that I should premise that it is in one of his many exegetical epistles that Jerome discusses this matter. A lady named Hedibia, inhabiting the furthest extremity of Gaul and known to Jerome only by the ardor of her piety, had sent to prove him with hard questions. He resolves her difficulties from Bethlehem; and I may be allowed to remind the reader of what is found to have been Jerome's practice on similar occasions—which, to judge from his writings, were of constant occurrence. In fact, Apodemius, who brought Jerome the twelve problems from Hedibia, brought him eleven more from a noble neighbor of hers, Algasia.

Once, when a single messenger had conveyed to him out of the African province a quantity of similar interrogatories, Jerome sent two Egyptian monks the following account of how he had proceeded in respect of the inquiry (it concerned I Cor. 15:51) which they had addressed to him: "Being pressed for time, I have presented you with the opinions of all the commentators, for the most part translating their very words, in order both to get rid of your questions and to put you in possession of ancient authorities on the subject."

This learned Father does not even profess to have been in the habit of delivering his own opinions or speaking his own sentiments on such occasions.

I claim to have established beyond the possibility of doubt or cavil that what we are here presented with is not the testimony of Jerome at all. It is evident that this learned Father amused himself with translating for the benefit of his Latin readers a part of the (lost) work of Eusebius (which, by the way, he is found to have possessed in the same abridged form in which it has come down to ourselves), and he seems to have regarded it as allowable to attribute to "Hedibia" the problems which he there met with. (He may perhaps have known that Eusebius before him had attributed them, with just a little reason, to "Marinus.")

In that age, for aught that appears to the contrary, it may have been regarded as a graceful compliment to address solutions of Scripture difficulties to persons of distinction—who possibly had never heard of those difficulties before—and even to represent the interrogatories which suggested them as originating with themselves. I offer this only in the way of suggestion and am not concerned to defend it. The only point I am concerned to establish is that Jerome is here a translator, not an original author—in other words, that it is Eusebius who here speaks, and not Jerome.

For a critic to pretend that it is in any sense the testimony of Jerome which we are here presented with, that Jerome is one of those Fathers "who, even though they copied from their predecessors, were yet competent to transmit the record of a fact," is entirely to misunderstand the case.

The man who translates—not adapts, but translates—the problem as well as its solution, who deliberately asserts that it emanated from a lady inhabiting the furthest extremity of Gaul, who nevertheless was demonstrably not its author, who goes on to propose as hers question after question verbatim as he found them written in the pages of Eusebius, and then resolves them one by one in the very

language of the same Father—such a writer has clearly conducted us into a region where his individual responsibility
quite disappears from sight. We must hear no more about
Jerome, therefore, as a witness against the genuineness of
the concluding verses of St. Mark's Gospel.

On the contrary. Proof is at hand that Jerome held these
verses to be genuine. The proper evidence of this is
supplied by the fact that he gave them a place in his revision
of the old Latin version of the Scriptures. If he had been
indeed persuaded of their absence from "almost all the
Greek codices," does any one imagine that he would have
suffered them to stand in the Vulgate? If he had met with
them in "scarcely any copies of the Gospel," do men really
suppose that he would yet have retained them?

To believe this would, again, be to forget what was the
known practice of this Father who, because he found the
expression "without a cause" ($\bar{e}ik\bar{e}$, St. Matt. 5:22) only
"in certain of his codices" but not "in the true one,"
omitted it from the Vulgate. Because, however, he read
"righteousness" (where we read "alms") in St. Matthew
6:1, he exhibits "justitiam" in his revision of the old Latin
version. On the other hand, though he knew of MSS (as he
expressly relates) which read "works" for "children"
($erg\bar{o}n$ for $tekn\bar{o}n$) in St. Matthew 6:19, he does not admit
that (manifestly corrupt) reading—which, however, is found
both in the Codex Vaticanus and the Codex Sinaiticus.

Let this suffice. I forbear to press the matter further. It
is an additional proof that Jerome accepted the conclusion
of St. Mark's Gospel that he actually quotes it, and on
more than one occasion; but to prove this, is to prove
more than is here required. I am concerned only to
demolish the assertion of Tischendorf, and Tregelles, and
Alford, and Davidson, and so many more, concerning the
testimony of Jerome; and I have demolished it. I pass on,
claiming to have shown that the name of Jerome as an
adverse witness must never again appear in this discussion.

Victor of Antioch

And from the familiar style in which this Father's name
is always introduced into the present discussion, no less
than from the invariable practice of assigning to him the
date A.D. 401, it might be supposed that Victor of
Antioch is a well-known personage. Yet is there scarcely a

commentator of antiquity about whom less is certainly known. Clinton (who enumerates 322 "Ecclesiastical Authors" from A.D. 70 to A.D. 685) does not even record his name. The recent *Dictionary of Greek and Roman Biography* is just as silent concerning him. Cramer (his latest editor) calls his very existence in question, proposing to attribute his commentary on St. Mark to Cyril of Alexandria.

Not to delay the reader needlessly, Victor of Antioch is an interesting and unjustly neglected Father of the Church, whose date (inasmuch as he apparently quotes sometimes from Cyril of Alexandria who died A.D. 444, and yet seems to have written soon after the death of Chrysostom, which took place A.D. 407) may be assigned to the first half of the fifth century—supposedly A.D. 425-450. And in citing him I shall always refer to the best (and most easily accessible) edition of his work, that of Cramer (1840) in the first volume of his *Catena.*

But a far graver charge is behind. From the confident air in which Victor's authority is appealed to by those who deem the last twelve verses of St. Mark's Gospel spurious, it would of course be inferred that his evidence is hostile to the verses in question; whereas his evidence to their genuineness is the most emphatic and extraordinary on record. Dr. Tregelles asserts that "his testimony" is the direct reverse of what Dr. Tregelles asserts it to be. This learned and respected critic has strangely misapprehended the evidence.

I must needs be brief in this place. I shall therefore confine myself to those facts concerning "Victor of Antioch," or rather concerning his work, which are necessary for the purpose in hand.

Now, his commentary on St. Mark's Gospel—as all must see who will be at the pains to examine it—is to a great extent a compilation. The same thing may be said, no doubt, to some extent, of almost every ancient commentary in existence. But I mean, concerning this particular work, that it proves to have been the author's plan not so much to give the general results of his acquaintance with the writings of Origen, Apollinarius, Theodorus of Mopsuestia, Eusebius, and Chrysostom, as—with or without acknowledgment—to transcribe largely (but with great license) from one or other of these writers.

Thus, the whole of his note on St. Mark 15:38, 39 is taken, without any hint that it is not original (much of it word for word), from Chrysostom's 88th Homily on St. Matthew's Gospel. The same is to be said of the first twelve lines of his note on St. Mark 16:9. On the other hand, the latter half of the note last mentioned professes to give the substance of what Eusebius had written on the same subject. It is in fact an extract from those very *"Quaestiones ad Marinum"* concerning which so much has been offered already.

All this, though it does not sensibly detract from the interest or the value of Victor's work, must be omitted entirely to change the character of his supposed evidence. He comes before us with a catena rather than a commentary, and as such in fact it is generally described. Quite plain is it, at all events, that the sentiments contained in the sections last referred to are not Victor's at all. For one half of them, no one but Chrysostom is responsible; for the other half, no one but Eusebius.

What then is the testimony of Victor? Does he offer any independent statement on the question in dispute, from which his own private opinion (though nowhere stated) may be lawfully inferred? Yes, indeed. Victor, though frequently a transcriber only, is observed every now and then to come forward in his own person and deliver his individual sentiment. But nowhere throughout his work does he deliver such remarkable testimony as in this place. Hear him!

"Notwithstanding that in very many copies of the present Gospel, the passage beginning, 'Now when (Jesus) was risen early the first day of the week, he appeared first to Mary Magdalene,' be not found (certain individuals having supposed it to be spurious)—yet we, at all events, inasmuch as in very many we have discovered it to exist, have, out of accurate copies, subjoined also the account of our Lord's ascension (following the words 'for they were afraid') in conformity with the Palestinian exemplar of Mark which exhibits the Gospel verity: that is to say, from the words, 'Now when (Jesus) was risen early the first day of the week,' &c., down to 'with signs following. Amen.' " And with these words Victor of Antioch brings his Commentary on St. Mark to an end.

Here then we find it roundly stated by a highly intelligent Father, writing in the first half of the fifth century—

1. that the reason why the last twelve verses of St. Mark are absent from some ancient copies of his Gospel is because they have been deliberately omitted by copyists;

2. that the ground for such omission was the subjective judgment of individuals, not the result of any appeal to documentary evidence. Victor, therefore, clearly held that the verses in question had been expunged in consequence of their (seeming) inconsistency with what is met with in the other Gospels;

3. that he, on the other hand, had convinced himself by reference to "very many" and "accurate" copies, that the verses in question are genuine;

4. that in particular the Palestinian Copy, which enjoyed the reputation of "exhibiting the genuine text of St. Mark," contained the verses in dispute. To opinion, therefore, Victor opposes authority. He makes his appeal to the most trustworthy documentary evidence with which he is acquainted; and the deliberate testimony which he delivers is a complete counterpoise and antidote to the loose phrases of Eusebius on the same subject;

5. that in consequence of all this, following the Palestinian exemplar, he had from accurate copies furnished his own work with the twelve verses in dispute—which is a categorical refutation of the statement frequently met with that the work of Victor of Antioch is without them.

We are now at liberty to sum up and to review the progress which has been hitherto made in this inquiry.

Six Fathers of the Church have been examined who are commonly represented as bearing hostile testimony to the last twelve verses of St. Mark's Gospel, and they have been easily reduced to one. Three of them (Hesychius, Jerome, Victor) prove to be echoes, not voices. The remaining two (Gregory of Nyssa and Severus) are neither voices nor echoes; but merely names; Gregory of Nyssa having really no more to do with this discussion than Philip of Macedon, and "Severus" and "Hesychius" representing one and the same individual. Only by a critic seeking to mislead his reader will any one of these five Fathers be in the future cited as witnessing against the genuineness of St. Mark

16:9-20.

Eusebius is the solitary witness who survives the ordeal of exact inquiry. But instead of proclaiming his distrust of this portion of the Gospel, Eusebius (as we have seen) enters on an elaborate proof that its contents are not inconsistent with what is found in the Gospels of St. Matthew and St. John. His testimony is reducible to two innocuous and wholly unconnected propositions: the first—that there existed in his day a vast number of copies in which the last chapter of St. Mark's Gospel ended abruptly at verse 8 (the correlative of which of course would be that there also existed a vast number which were furnished with the present ending); the second—that by putting a comma after the word *Anastas,* St. Mark 16:9 is capable of being reconciled with St. Matthew 28:1. . . . I profess myself unable to understand how it can be pretended that Eusebius would have subscribed to the opinions of Tischendorf, Tregelles, and the rest, that the Gospel of St. Mark was never finished by its inspired author or was mutilated before it came abroad; at all events, that the last twelve verses are spurious.

The observations of Eusebius are found to have been adopted and in part transcribed by an unknown writer of the sixth century—whether Hesychius or Severus is not certainly known; but if it were Hesychius, then it was not Severus; if Severus, then not Hesychius.

This writer, however (whoever he may have been), is careful to convince us that individually he entertained no doubt whatever about the genuineness of this part of Scripture; for he says that he writes in order to remove the (hypothetical) objections of others and to silence their (imaginary) doubts. Nay, he freely quotes the verses as genuine and declares that they were read in his day on a certain Sunday night in the public service of the church. . . .

To represent such a one (it matters nothing, I repeat, whether we call him "Hesychius of Jerusalem" or "Severus of Antioch") as a hostile witness is simply to misrepresent the facts of the case. He is, on the contrary, the strenuous champion of the verses which he is commonly represented as impugning.

As for Jerome, since that illustrious Father comes before us in this place as a translator of Eusebius only, he is no more responsible for what Eusebius says concerning St. Mark 16:9-20 than Hobbes of Malmesbury is responsible for anything that Thucydides has related concerning the Peloponnesian War. Individually, however, it is certain that Jerome was convinced of the genuineness of St. Mark 16:9-20; for in two different places of his writings he not only quotes the 9th and 14th verses, but he exhibits all the twelve in the Vulgate.

Lastly, Victor of Antioch, who wrote in an age when Eusebius was held to be an infallible oracle on points of biblical criticism—having dutifully rehearsed, (like the rest) the feeble expedient of that illustrious Father for harmonizing St. Mark 16:9 with the narrative of St. Matthew—is observed to cite the statements of Eusebius concerning the last twelve verses of St. Mark only in order to refute them. Not that he opposes opinion to opinion (for the opinions of Eusebius and of Victor of Antioch on this behalf were probably identical), but the statement he meets with counter statement, fact he confronts with fact. Scarcely can anything be imagined more emphatic or more conclusive than his testimony.

For the reader is requested to observe that here is an ecclesiastic, writing in the first half of the fifth century, who expressly witnesses to the genuineness of the verses in dispute. He had made reference, he says, and ascertained their existence in very many MSS (*hōs en pleistois*). He had derived his text from "accurate" ones: *ex akribōn antigraphōn*. More than that: he leads his reader to infer that he had personally resorted to the famous Palestinian Copy, the text of which was held to exhibit the inspired verity, and had satisfied himself that the concluding section of St. Mark's Gospel was there.

He had, therefore, been either to Jerusalem or else to Caesarea, had inquired for those venerable records which had once belonged to Origen and Pamphilus, and had inspected them. Testimony more express, more weighty—I was going to say, more decisive—can scarcely be imagined. It may with truth be said to close the present discussion.

With this, in fact, Victor lays down his pen. So also may I. I submit that nothing whatever which has hitherto come before us lends the slightest countenance to the modern dream that St. Mark's Gospel, as it left the hands of its inspired author, ended abruptly at verse 8. Neither

Eusebius nor Jerome, neither Severus of Antioch nor Hesychius of Jerusalem, certainly not Victor of Antioch, least of all Gregory of Nyssa yield a particle of support to that monstrous fancy. The notion is an invention, a pure imagination of the critics ever since the days of Griesbach.

It remains to ascertain what is the evidence of the MSS on this subject. And the MSS require to be the more attentively studied, because it is to them that our opponents are accustomed most confidently to appeal. On them in fact they rely. The nature and the value of the most ancient manuscript testimony available will be scrupulously investigated in the next two chapters.

Manuscript Testimony Shown to Be Overwhelmingly in Favor of These Verses

The two oldest copies of the Gospels in existence are the famous codex in the Vatican Library at Rome, known as Codex B, and the codex which Tischendorf brought from Mt. Sinai in 1859, which he designates by the first letter of the Hebrew alphabet (aleph). These two manuscripts are probably not of equal antiquity. An interval of fifty years at least seems to be required to account for the marked difference between them. If the first belongs to the beginning, the second may be referred to the middle or latter part of the fourth century. But the two manuscripts agree in this, that they are without the last twelve verses of St. Mark's Gospel. In both, after *ephobounto gar* (v. 8), comes the subscription: in Codex B, ΚΑΤΑ ΜΑΡΚΟΝ; in Codex Aleph ΕΥΑΓΓΕΛΙΟΝ ΚΑΤΑ ΜΑΡΚΟΝ.

Let it not be supposed that we have any more facts of this class to produce. All has been stated. It is not that the evidence of manuscripts is one, the evidence of Fathers and versions another. The very reverse is the case. Manuscripts, Fathers, and versions alike are only not unanimous in bearing consistent testimony, but the consentient witness of the MSS is even extraordinary. With the exception of the two uncial MSS which have just been named, there is not one codex in existence, uncial or cursive (and we are acquainted with, at least, eighteen other uncials, and about six hundred cursive copies of this Gospel), which leaves out the last twelve verses of St. Mark.

The inference which an unscientific observer would draw from this fact is no doubt in this instance the correct one. He demands to be shown the Alexandrine (A) and the Parisian Codex (C)—neither of them probably removed by much more than fifty years from the date of the Codex Sinaiticus, and both unquestionably derived from different originals—and he ascertains that no countenance is lent by either of those venerable monuments to the proposed omission of this part of the sacred text.

He discovers that the Codex Bezae (D), the only remaining very ancient MS authority—notwithstanding that it is observed on most occasions to exhibit an extraordinary sympathy with the Vatican (B)—here sides with A and C against B and Aleph. He inquires after all the other uncials and all the cursive MSS in existence (some of them dating from the tenth century) and requests to have it explained to him why it is to be supposed that all these many witnesses—belonging to so many different patriarchates, provinces, ages of the Church—have entered into a grand conspiracy to bear false witness on a point of this magnitude and importance? But he obtains no intelligible answer to this question.

How, then, is an unprejudiced student to draw any inference but one from the premises? That single peculiarity (he tells himself) of bringing the second Gospel abruptly to a close at the 8th verse of the 16th chapter is absolutely fatal to the two codices in question. It is useless to din into his ears that those codices are probably both of the fourth century, unless men are prepared to add the assurance that a codex of the fourth century is of necessity a more trustworthy witness to the text of the Gospels than a codex of the fifth.

The omission of these twelve verses, I repeat, in itself destroys his confidence in Codex B and Codex Aleph; for it is obvious that a copy of the Gospels which has been so seriously mutilated in one place may have been slightly tampered with in another. He is willing to suspend his judgment, of course. The two oldest copies of the Gospels in existence are entitled to great reverence because of their high antiquity. They must be allowed a most patient, most unprejudiced, most respectful, nay, a most indulgent hearing. But when all this has been freely accorded, on no intelligible principle can more be claimed for any two MSS in the world.

The rejoinder to all this is sufficiently obvious. Mistrust

will no doubt have been thrown over the evidence borne to the text of Scripture in a thousand other places by Codex B and Codex Aleph after demonstration that those two codices exhibit a mutilated text in the present place. But what else is this but the very point requiring demonstration? Why may not these two be right, and all the other MSS wrong?

I propose, therefore, that we reverse the process. Proceed we to examine the evidence borne by these two witnesses on certain other occasions which admit of no difference of opinion, or next to none. Let us endeavor, I say, to ascertain the character of the witnesses by a patient and unprejudiced examination of their evidence—not in one place—and throughout. If we find it invariably consentient and invariably truthful, then of course a mighty presumption will have been established, the very strongest possible, that their adverse testimony in respect of the conclusion of St. Mark's Gospel must needs be worthy of all acceptation.

But if, on the contrary, our inquiries will conduct us to the very opposite result, what else can happen but that our confidence in these two MSS will be hopelessly shaken? We must in such case be prepared to admit that it is just as likely as not that this is only one more occasion on which these "two false witnesses" have conspired to witness falsely.

If, at this juncture, extraneous evidence of an entirely trustworthy kind can be procured to confront them— above all, if some one ancient witness of unimpeachable veracity can be found who will bear contradictory evidence—what other alternative will be left us but to reject their testimony in respect of St. Mark 16:9-20 with something like indignation; and to acquiesce in the belief of universal Christendom for eighteen hundred years that these twelve verses are just as much entitled to our unhesitating acceptance as any other twelve verses in the Gospel which can be named?

It is undeniable, in the meantime, that for the last quarter of a century it has become the fashion to demand for the readings of Codex B something very like absolute deference. The grounds for this superstitious sentiment (for really I can describe it in no apter way) I profess myself unable to discover. Codex B comes to us without a history: without recommendation of any kind, except that of its antiquity. It bears traces of careless transcription in every page. The mistakes which the original transcriber made are of perpetual recurrence.

In the Gospels alone, Codex B leaves out words or whole clauses no less than 1,491 times, of which by far the largest proportion is found in St. Mark's Gospel. Many of these, no doubt, are to be accounted for by the proximity of a "like ending." The Vatican MS (like the Sinaitic) was originally derived from an older codex which contained about twelve or thirteen letters in a line.

And it will be found that some of its omissions which have given rise to prolonged discussion are probably to be referred to nothing else but the oscitancy of a transcriber with such a codex before him: without having recourse to any more abstruse hypothesis; without any imputation of bad faith; certainly without supposing that the words omitted did not exist in the inspired autograph of the Evangelist.

But then it is undeniable that some of the omissions in Codex B are not to be so explained. On the other hand, I can testify to the fact that the codex is disfigured throughout with repetitions. The original scribe is often found to have not only written the same words twice over, but to have failed whenever he did so to take any notice with his pen of what he had done.

What, then (I must again inquire), are the grounds for the superstitious reverence which is entertained in certain quarters for the readings of Codex B? If it be a secret known to the recent editors of the New Testament, they have certainly contrived to keep it wondrously close.

More recently, a claim to coordinate primacy has been set up on behalf of the Codex Sinaiticus. Tischendorf is actually engaged in remodeling his seventh Leipsig edition, chiefly in conformity with the readings of his lately discovered MS. And yet the codex in question abounds with "errors of the eye and pen, to an extent not unparalleled, but happily rather unusual in documents of first-rate importance."

On many occasions, ten, twenty, thirty, forty, words are dropped through very carelessness. "Letters and words, even whole sentences, are frequently written twice over, or begun and immediately cancelled: while that gross blunder

... whereby a clause is omitted because it happens to end in the same words as the clause preceding, occurs no less times than 115 in the New Testament. Tregelles has freely pronounced that 'the state of the text, as proceeding from the first scribe, may be regarded as very rough.' "

But when "the first scribe" and his "very rough" performance have been thus unceremoniously disposed of, one would like to be informed what remains to command respect in Codex Aleph? Is, then, manuscript authority to be confounded with editorial caprice, exercising itself on the corrections of "at least ten different revisers," who, from the sixth to the seventh century, have been endeavoring to lick into shape a text which its original author left "very rough"?

The coordinate primacy (as I must needs call it) which, within the last few years, has been claimed for Codex B and Codex Aleph threatens to grow into a species of tyranny, from which I venture to predict there will come in the end an unreasonable and unsalutary recoil. It behooves us, therefore, to look closely into this matter and to require a reason for what is being done. The text of the sacred deposit is far too precious a thing to be sacrificed to an irrational or at least a superstitious devotion to two MSS simply because they may possibly be older by a hundred years than any other which we possess.

How ready the most recent editors of the New Testament have shown themselves to hammer the sacred text on the anvil of Codices B and Aleph—not unfrequently in defiance of the evidence of all other MSS and sometimes to the serious detriment of the deposit—would admit of striking illustration were this the place for such details. Tischendorf's English "New Testament"—"with various readings from the three most celebrated manuscripts of the Greek text" translated at the foot of every page—is a recent attempt (1869) to popularize the doctrine that we have to look exclusively to two or three of the oldest copies if we would possess the Word of God in its integrity. Dean Alford's constant appeal in his revision of the Authorized Version (1870) to "the oldest MSS" (meaning thereby generally Codices Aleph and B with one or two others) is an abler endeavor to familiarize the public mind with the same belief. I am bent on showing that there is nothing whatever in the character of either of the codices in question to warrant this servile deference.

And first, ought it not sensibly to detract from our opinion of the value of their evidence to discover that it is easier to find two consecutive verses in which the two MSS differ, the one from the other, than two consecutive verses in which they entirely agree? Now this is a plain matter of fact, of which any one who pleases may easily convince himself. But the character of two witnesses who habitually contradict one another has been accounted, in every age, precarious. On every such occasion, only one of them can possibly be speaking the truth. Shall I be thought unreasonable if I confess that these perpetual inconsistencies between codices B and Aleph—grave inconsistencies and occasionally even gross ones—altogether destroy my confidence in either?

On the other hand, discrepant as the testimony of these two MSS is throughout, they yet, strange to say, conspire every here and there in exhibiting minute corruptions of such a unique and peculiar kind as to betray a (probably not very remote) common corrupt original. These coincidences in fact are so numerous and so extraordinary as to establish a real connection between those two codices; and that connection is fatal to any claim which might be set up on their behalf as wholly independent witnesses.

Further, it is evident that both alike have been subjected, probably during the process of transcription, to the same depraving influences. But because such statements require to be established by an induction of instances, the reader's attention must now be invited to a few samples of the grave blemishes which disfigure our two oldest copies of the Gospel.

And first, since it is the omission of the end of St. Mark's Gospel which has given rise to the present discussion, it becomes a highly significant circumstance that the original scribe of Codex Aleph had also omitted the end of the Gospel According to St. John. In this suppression of verse 25, Codex Aleph stands alone among MSS. A cloud of primitive witnesses vouch for the genuineness of the verse. Surely, it is nothing else but the *reductio ad absurdum* of a theory of recension (with Tischendorf in his last edition) to accommodate our printed text to the vicious standard of the original penman of Codex Aleph and bring the last chapter of St. John's Gospel to a close at verse 24!

Codex B, on the other hand, omits the whole of those two solemn verses wherein St. Luke describes our Lord's "agony and bloody sweat," together with the act of the ministering angel. As to the genuineness of those verses, recognized as they are by Justin Martyr, Irenaeus, Hippolytus, Epiphadoret, by all the oldest versions, and by almost every MS in existence, including Codex Aleph—it admits of no doubt.

Here from the Gospel in the oldest of the uncials there is no need whatever to resort to the hypothesis that such portions of "the admitted error of Codex B in this place," to quote the words of Scrivener, "ought to make some of its advocates more chary of their confidence in cases where it is less countenanced by other witnesses than in the instance before us."

Codex B (not Codex Aleph) is further guilty of the "grave error" (as Dean Alford justly styles it) of omitting that solemn record of the Evangelist: "Then said Jesus, Father, forgive them; for they know not what they do." It also withholds the statement that the inscription on the cross was "in letters of Greek, and Latin, and Hebrew." Codex Aleph, on the other hand, omits the confession of the man born blind in St. John 9:38.

But the inspired text has been depraved in the same licentious way throughout by the "responsible" authors of Codex B and Codex Aleph, although such corruptions have attracted little notice from their comparative unimportance.

We are by this time in a condition to form a truer estimate of the value of the testimony borne by these two manuscripts in respect of the last twelve verses of St. Mark's Gospel. If we were disposed before to regard their omission of an important passage as a serious matter, we certainly cannot any longer so regard it. We have by this time seen enough to disabuse our minds of every prejudice. Codices B and Aleph are the very reverse of infallible guides. Their deflections from the truth of Scripture are more constant, as well as more licentious by far, than those of their younger brethren; their unauthorized omissions from the sacred text are not only far more frequent but far more flagrant also. And yet the main matter before us—their omission of the last twelve verses of St. Mark's Gospel—when rightly understood proves to be an entirely different phenomenon from what an ordinary reader might have been led to suppose. Attention is specially requested for the remarks which follow.

It is true to say that in the Vatican Codex (B), which is unquestionably the oldest we possess, St. Mark's Gospel ends abruptly at the 8th verse of the 16th chapter and that the customary subscription *(KATA MAPKON)* follows; but it is far from being the whole truth. It requires to be stated in addition that the scribe, whose plan is found to have been to begin every fresh book of the Bible at the top of the next ensuing column to that which contained the concluding words of the preceding book, has at the close of St. Mark's Gospel deviated from his else invariable practice.

He has left in this place one column entirely vacant. It is the only vacant column in the whole manuscript—a blank space abundantly sufficient to contain the twelve verses which he nevertheless withheld.

Why did he leave that column vacant? What can have induced the scribe on this solitary occasion to depart from his established rule? The phenomenon (I believe I was the first to call distinct attention to it) is in the highest degree significant and admits of only one interpretation.

The older MS from which Codex B was copied must have infallibly contained the twelve verses in dispute. The copyist was instructed to leave them out, and he obeyed; but he prudently left a blank space *in memoriam rei.* Never was blank more intelligible! Never was silence more eloquent!

By this simple expedient, strange to relate, the Vatican Codex is made to refute itself even while it seems to be bearing testimony against the concluding verses of St. Mark's Gospel by withholding them; for it forbids the inference which, under ordinary circumstances, must have been drawn from that omission.

It does more. By leaving room for the verses it omits, it brings into prominent notice at the end of fifteen centuries and a half a more ancient witness than itself. The venerable author of the original codex from which Codex B was copied is thereby brought to view. And thus, our supposed adversary (Codex B) proves our most useful ally; for it procures us the testimony of a hitherto unsuspected witness.

The earlier scribe, I repeat, unmistakably comes forward at this stage of the inquiry to explain that he at least is prepared to answer for the genuineness of these twelve concluding verses with which the later scribe, his copyist, from his omission of them might unhappily be thought to have been unacquainted.

It will be perceived that nothing is gained by suggesting that the scribe of Codex B may have copied from a MS which exhibited the same phenomenon which he has himself reproduced. This, by shifting the question a little further back, does but make the case against Codex Aleph the stronger.

But in truth, after the revelation which has been already elicited from Codex B, the evidence of Codex Aleph may be very summarily disposed of. I have already, on independent grounds, ventured to assign to that codex a somewhat later date than is claimed for the Codex Vaticanus. My opinion is confirmed by observing that the Sinaitic contains no such blank space at the end of St. Mark's Gospel as is conspicuous in the Vatican Codex. I infer that the Sinaitic was copied from a codex which had been already mutilated and reduced to the condition of Codex B, and that the scribe—only because he knew not what it meant—exhibited St. Mark's Gospel in consequence as if it really had no claim to those twelve concluding verses which, nevertheless, every authority we have hitherto met with has affirmed to belong to it of right.

Whatever may be thought of the foregoing suggestion, it is at least undeniable that Codex B and Codex Aleph are at variance on the main point. They contradict one another concerning the twelve concluding verses of St. Mark's Gospel. For while Codex Aleph refuses to know anything at all about those verses, Codex B admits that it remembers them well by volunteering the statement that they were found in the older codex, of which it is in every other respect a faithful representative. The older and the better manuscript (B), therefore, refutes its junior (Aleph). And it will be seen that logically this brings the inquiry to a close, as far as the evidence of the manuscripts is concerned. We have referred to the oldest extant copy of the Gospels in order to obtain its testimony; and, "though without the twelve verses concerning which you are so solicitous," it seems to say, "I yet hesitate not to confess to you that an older copy than myself—the ancient codex from which I was copied—actually did contain them."

The problem may, in fact, be briefly stated as follows. Of the four oldest codices of the Gospels extant—B, Aleph, A, C—two (B and Aleph) are without these twelve verses and two (A and C) are with them. Are these twelve verses then an unauthorized addition to A and C, or are they an unwarrantable omission from B and Aleph? B itself declares plainly that from itself they are an omission. And B is the oldest codex of the Gospel in existence. What candid mind will persist in clinging to the solitary fact that from the single Codex Aleph these verses are away, in proof that "St. Mark's Gospel was at first without the verses which at present conclude it"?

Let others decide, therefore, whether the present discussion has not already reached a stage at which an unprejudiced arbiter might be expected to address the prosecuting parties somewhat to the following effect:

"This case must now be dismissed. The charge brought by yourselves against these verses was that they are an unauthorized addition to the second Gospel, a spurious appendix of which the Evangelist St. Mark can have known nothing. But so far from substantiating this charge, you have not adduced a single particle of evidence which renders it even probable.

"The appeal was made by yourselves to Fathers and to MSS. It has been accepted. And with what result?

"Those many Fathers whom you represented as hostile prove on investigation to be reducible to one, viz. Eusebius; and Eusebius, as we have seen, does not say that the verses are spurious but on the contrary labors hard to prove that they may very well be genuine. On the other hand, there are earlier Fathers than Eusebius who quote them without any signs of misgiving. In this way, the positive evidence in their favor is carried back to the second century.

"Declining the testimony of the versions, you insisted on an appeal to MSS. On the MSS, in fact, you still make your stand—or rather you rely on the oldest of them; for (as you are aware) every MS in the world except the two oldest are against you.

"I have therefore questioned the elder of those two MSS, and it has volunteered the avowal that an older MS than itself—the codex from which it was copied was furnished with those very verses which you wish me to believe that some older MS still must needs have been without. What else can be said, then, of your method but that it is frivolous? and of your charge, but that it is contradicted by the evidence to which you yourselves appeal?

"But it is illogical; that is, it is unreasonable, besides.

"For it is high time to point out that even if it so happened that the oldest known MS was observed to be without these twelve concluding verses, it would still remain a thing unproved (not to say highly improbable) that from the autograph of the Evangelist himself they were also away.

"Supposing, further, that no ecclesiastical writer of the second or third century could be found who quoted them; even so, it would not follow that there existed no such verses for a primitive Father to quote. The earliest of the versions might in addition yield faltering testimony; but even so, who would be so rash as to raise on such a slender basis the monstrous hypothesis that St. Mark's Gospel when it left the hands of its inspired author was without the verses which at present conclude it? How, then, would you have proposed to account for the consistent testimony of an opposite kind yielded by every other known document in the world?

"But, on the other hand, what are the facts of the case? (1) The earliest of the Fathers, (2) the most venerable of the versions, (3) the oldest MS of which we can obtain any tidings—all are observed to recognize these verses. *'Cadit Quaestio'* therefore. The last shadow of pretext has vanished for maintaining with Tischendorf that 'Mark the Evangelist knew nothing of' these verses; with Tregelles that 'The Book of Mark itself extends no further than *ephobounto gar;* with Griesbach that 'the last leaf of the original Gospel was probably torn away.'... It is high time, I say, that this case were dismissed. But there are also costs to be paid. Codex B and Codex Aleph are convicted of being 'two false witnesses' and must be held to go forth from this inquiry with an injured reputation."

This entire subject is of so much importance that I must needs yet awhile crave the reader's patience and attention.

Further Manuscript Testimony

The subject which exclusively occupied our attention throughout the foregoing section admits of apt and powerful illustration. Its vast importance will be a sufficient apology for the particular disquisition which follows, and might have been spared, but for the plain challenge of the famous critic to be named immediately.

"There are two remarkable readings," says Tischendorf, addressing English readers on this subject in 1868, "which are very instructive toward determining the age of the manuscripts [Aleph and B] and their authority." He proceeds to adduce the absence from both [manuscripts] of the last twelve verses of St. Mark's Gospel, concerning which the reader probably thinks that by this time he has heard enough. Next, he appeals to their omission of the words *en Ephesōi* from the first verse of St. Paul's Epistle to the Ephesians, another peculiarity in which Codices Aleph and B stand quite alone among MSS.

Here is an extraordinary note of sympathy between two copies of the New Testament indeed. Altogether unique is it, and no one will deny that it powerfully corroborates the general opinion of their high antiquity. But how about "their authority"? Does the coincidence also raise our opinion of the trustworthiness of the text which these two MSS concur in exhibiting? For that is the question which has to be considered—the only question. The ancientness of a reading is one thing, its genuineness (as I have explained elsewhere) quite another. The questions are entirely distinct. It may even be added that while the one is really of little moment, the latter is of all the importance in the world.

I am saying that it matters very little whether Codices Aleph and B were written in the beginning of the fourth century or in the beginning of the fifth; whereas it matters much, or rather it matters everything, whether they exhibit the Word of God faithfully, or occasionally with scandalous license.

Tischendorf—the illustrious discoverer and champion of Codex Aleph, and who is accustomed to appeal triumphantly to its omission of the words *en Ephesōi* as the other conclusive proof of the trustworthiness of its text—may be presumed to be the most able advocate it is likely to meet with, as well as the man best acquainted with what is to be urged in its support. From him, we learn that the evidence for the omission of the words in question is as follows: "In the beginning of the Epistle to the Ephesians we read, 'to the saints which are at Ephesus'; but Marcion (A.D. 130-140) did not find the words 'at Ephesus' in his copy.

"The same is true of Origen (A.D. 185-254); and Basil the Great (who died A.D. 379) affirmed that those words were wanting in old copies. And this omission accords very well with the encyclical or general character of the epistle. At the present day, our ancient Greek MSS and all ancient versions contain the words 'at Ephesus'; yea *(sic),* even Jerome knew no copy with a different reading. Now, only the Sinaitic and the Vatican correspond with the old copies of Basil, and those of Origen and Marcion." This, then, is the sum of the evidence. Proceed we to examine it somewhat in detail.

And first, I take leave to point out that the learned writer is absolutely without authority for his assertion that "Marcion did not find the words *en Ephesōi* in his copy" of St. Paul's Epistle to the Ephesians. Tischendorf's one pretense for saying so is Tertullian's statement that certain heretics (Marcion he specifies by name) had given to St. Paul's Epistle to the Ephesians the unauthorized title of "Epistle to the Laodiceans."

This (argues Tischendorf) Marcion could not have done had he found *en Ephesōi* in the first verse. But the proposed inference is clearly invalid. For, with what show of reason can Marcion—whom Tertullian taxes with having dared *"titulum interpolare"* in the case of St. Paul's Epistle to the Ephesians—be therefore assumed to have read the first verse differently from ourselves? Rather is the directly opposite inference suggested by the very language in which Tertullian (who after all does but say that Marcion and his crew feigned concerning St. Paul's Epistle to the Ephesians, that it was addressed to the Laodiceans)—and betake themselves to the pages of Epiphanius, who lived about a century and a half later.

This Father had for many years made Marcion's work his special study and has elaborately described it, as well as presented us with copious extracts from it. And the account in Epiphanius proves that Tischendorf is mistaken in the statement which he addressed to the English reader (quoted above) and that he would have better consulted for his reputation if he had kept to the *"ut videtur"* with which (in his edition of 1859) he originally broached his opinion. It proved in fact to be no matter of opinion at all.

Epiphanius states distinctly that the Epistle to the Ephesians was one of the ten epistles of St. Paul which Marcion retained. In his *"Apostolicon,"* or collection of the (mutilated) Apostolical Epistles, the "Epistle to the Ephesians" (identified by the considerable quotations which Epiphanius makes from it) stood (he says) seventh in order; while the (so-called) "Epistle to the Laodiceans"—a distinct composition therefore—had the eleventh, that is, the last place assigned to it.

That this latter epistle contained a corrupt exhibition of Ephesians 4:5 is true enough. Epiphanius records the fact in two places. But then it is to be borne in mind that he charges Marcion with having derived that quotation from the apocryphal Epistle to the Laodiceans instead of taking it, as he ought to have done, from the genuine Epistle to the Ephesians. The passage when faithfully exhibited (as Epiphanius points out) by its very form refutes the heretical tenet which the context of Marcion's spurious Epistle to the Laodiceans was intended to establish, and which the verse in question, in its interpolated form, might seem to favor.

I have entered into this whole question more in detail perhaps than was necessary, but I was determined to prove that Tischendorf's statement that "Marcion (A.D. 130-140) did not find the words 'at Ephesus' in his copy" is absolutely without foundation. It is even contradicted by the known facts of the case. By and by I shall have something more to say about Marcion—who, it is quite certain, read the text of Ephesians 1:1 exactly as we do.

The only Father who so expresses himself as to warrant the inference that the words *en Ephesōi* were absent from his copy is Origen, in the beginning of the third century. "Only in the case of the Ephesians," he writes, "do we meet with the expression 'the saints which are'; and we inquire: unless that additional phrase be simply redundant, what can it possibly signify?

"Consider, then, whether those who have been partakers of His nature who revealed Himself to Moses by the Name of I AM, may not, in consequence of such union with Him, be designated as 'those which are': persons called out of a state of not-being, so to speak, into a state of being."

If Origen had read *tois hagiois tois ousin Ephesōi* in his copy, it is to me incredible that he would have gone so very far out of his way to miss the sense of such a plain, and in fact, unmistakable expression.

Bishop Middleton, and Michaelis before him, reasoning however only from the place in Basil (to be quoted immediately), are unwilling to allow that the words *en Ephesōi* were ever away from the text. It must be admitted as the obvious inference from what Jerome has delivered on this subject that he, too, seems to know nothing of the reading (if reading it can be called) of Codices B and Aleph.

Learned men have tasked their ingenuity to account for the phenomenon on which we have been bestowing so many words. The endeavor is commendable; but I take leave to remark in passing that if we are to set about discovering reasons at the end of fifteen hundred years for every corrupt reading which found its way into the sacred text during the first three centuries subsequent to the death of St. John, we shall have enough to do.

Let any one take up the Codex Bezae (with which, by the way, Codex B shows marvelous sympathy) and explain if he can why there is a grave omission, or else a gross interpolation, in almost every page; and how it comes to pass that Codex D "reproduces the *'textus receptus'* of the Acts much in the same way that one of the best Chaldee Targums does the Hebrew of the Old Testament; so wide are the variations in the diction, so constant and inveterate the practice of expounding the narrative by means of interpolations which seldom recommend themselves as genuine by even a semblance of internal probability."

Our business as critics is not to invent theories to account for the errors of copyists but rather to ascertain where they have erred, where not. What with the inexcusable depravations of early heretics, the preposterous emendations of ancient critics, the injudicious assiduity of harmonizers, the licentious caprice of individuals; what with errors resulting from the inopportune recollection of similar or parallel places, or from the familiar phraseology of the ecclesiastical lections, or from the inattention of scribes, or from marginal glosses; however arising, endless are the corrupt readings of the oldest MSS in existence, and it is by no means safe to follow up the detection of a depravation of the text with a theory to account for its existence. Let me be allowed to say that such theories are seldom satisfactory. Guesses only they are at best.

Let it be declared without offense, that there appears to exist in the mind of this illustrious critic (Tischendorf) a hopeless confusion between the antiquity of a codex and the value of its readings. I venture to assert that a reading is valuable or the contrary exactly in proportion to the probability of its being true or false. Interesting it is sure to be, be what it may, if it be found in a very ancient codex—interesting and often instructive; but the editor of Scripture must needs bring every reading, wherever found, to this test at last: is it to be thought that what I am here presented with is what the Evangelist or the apostle actually wrote?

If an answer in the negative be obtained to this question, then the fact that one, or two, or three of the early Fathers appear to have so read the place will not avail to impart to the rejected reading one particle of value. And yet Tischendorf thinks it enough in all the preceding passages to assure his reader that a given reading in Codex Aleph was recognized by Origen, by Tertullian, by Jerome. To have established this one point he evidently thinks sufficient.

There is implied in all this an utterly false major premise, namely, that scriptural quotations found in the writings of Origen, Tertullian, and Jerome must needs be the *ipsissima verba* of the Spirit. Instead, it is notorious "that the worst corruptions to which the New Testament has ever been subjected originated within a hundred years after it was composed: that Irenaeus and the whole Western, with a portion of the Syrian Church, used far inferior manuscripts to those employed by Stunica, or Erasmus, or Stephens, thirteen centuries later, when molding the Textus Receptus."

And one is astonished that a critic of so much sagacity (who of course knows better) should deliberately put forth so gross a fallacy—not only without a word of explanation, a word of caution, but in such a manner as inevitably to mislead an unsuspecting reader. Without offense to Dr.

Tischendorf, I must be allowed to declare that, in the remarks we have been considering, he shows himself far more bent on glorifying the Codex Sinaiticus than in establishing the truth of the pure Word of God. He convinces me that to have found an early uncial codex is every bit as fatal as to have "taken a gift." Verily "it doth blind the eyes of the wise."

And with this, I shall conclude my remarks on these two famous codices. I humbly record my deliberate conviction that when the science of textual criticism, which is at present only in its infancy, comes to be better understood (and a careful collation of every existing codex of the New Testament is one indispensable preliminary to its being ever placed on a trustworthy basis), a very different estimate will be formed of the importance of not a few of those readings which at present are received with unquestioning submission, chiefly on the authority of Codex B and Codex Aleph.

On the other hand, it is perfectly certain that no future collations, no future discoveries will ever make it credible that the last twelve verses of St. Mark's Gospel are a spurious supplement to the evangelical narrative or that the words *en Ephesōi* are an unauthorized interpolation of the inspired text.

The Purport of Ancient Scholia, and Notes in MSS on the Subject of These Verses, Shown to Be the Reverse of What Is Commonly Supposed

In the present section I propose to pass under review whatever manuscript testimony still remains unconsidered, our attention having been hitherto exclusively devoted to Codices B and Aleph. True, that the rest of the evidence may be disposed of in a single short sentence: The twelve verses under discussion are found in every copy of the Gospels in existence with the exception of Codices B and Aleph.

But then, we are assured (by Dr. Tregelles, for example) that "a note or a scholion stating the absence of these verses from many, from most, or from the most correct copies (often from Victor or Severus) is found in twenty-five other cursive codices." Tischendorf has nearly the same words: "Scholia in very many MSS state that the Gospel of Mark in the most ancient (and most accurate) copies ended at the ninth verse." That distinguished critic supports his assertion by appealing to seven MSS in particular and referring generally to "about twenty-five others." Dr. Davidson adopts every word of this blindfolded.

Now of course if all that precedes were true, this department of the evidence would become deserving of serious attention. But I simply deny the fact. I entirely deny that the "note or scholion" which these learned persons affirm to be of such frequent occurrence has any existence whatever, except in their own imaginations. On the other hand, I assert that notes or scholia which state the exact reverse (viz., that "in the older" or "the more accurate copies" the last twelve verses of St. Mark's Gospel are contained) recur even perpetually.

The plain truth is this: These eminent persons have taken their information second-hand—partly from Griesbach, partly from Scholz—without suspicion and without inquiry. But then they have slightly misrepresented Scholz; and Scholz (1830) slightly misunderstood Griesbach; and Greisbach (1796) took liberties with Wetstein; and Wetstein (1751) made a few serious mistakes.

The consequence might have been anticipated. The truth, once thrust out of sight, has been usurped by certain erroneous statements which every succeeding critic now reproduces, evidently to his own entire satisfaction, though not (it must be declared) altogether to his own credit. Let me be allowed to explain in detail what has occurred.

Griesbach is found to have pursued the truly German plan of setting down all the twenty-five MSS and all the five patristic authorities which up to this time had been cited as bearing on the genuineness of St. Mark 16:9-20. He gives the former in numerical order, stating generally concerning them that in one or other of those authorities it would be found recorded "that the verses in question were anciently wanting in some, or in most, or in almost all the Greek copies, or in the most accurate ones; or else that they were found in a few, or in the more accurate copies, or in many, or in most of them, specially in the Palestinian Gospel."

The learned writer (who had made up his mind long

before that the verses in question are to be rejected) no doubt perceived that this would be the most convenient way of disposing of the evidence for and against; but one is at a loss to understand how English scholars can have acquiesced in such a slipshod statement for well nigh a hundred years. A very little study of the subject would have shown them that Griesbach derived the first eleven of his references from Wetstein, the last fourteen from Birch. As for Scholz, he unsuspiciously adopted Griesbach's fatal enumeration of codices, adding five to the number and only interrupting the series here and there, in order to insert the quotations which Wetstein had already supplied from certain of them.

With Scholz, therefore, rests the blame for everything which has been written since 1830 concerning the MS evidence for this part of St. Mark's Gospel subsequent critics having been content to adopt his statements without acknowledgment and without examination. Unfortunately Scholz did his work (as usual) in such a slovenly style, that besides perpetuating old mistakes he invented new ones—which, of course, have been reproduced by those who have simply translated or transcribed him. And now I shall examine his note "(z)", with which practically all that has since been delivered on this subject by Tischendorf, Tregelles, Davidson, and the rest, is identical.

Scholz (copying Griesbach) first states that in two MSS in the Vatican Library the verses in question "are marked with an asterisk." The original author of this statement was Birch, who followed it up by explaining the fatal signification of this mark. From that day to this, the asterisks in Codices Vaticanus 756 and 757 have been religiously reproduced by every critic in turn; and it is universally taken for granted that they represent two ancient witnesses against the genuineness of the last twelve verses of the Gospel According to St. Mark.

And yet (let me say it without offense) a very little attention ought to be enough to convince anyone familiar with this subject that the proposed inference is absolutely inadmissible. For, in the first place, a solitary asterisk (not at all a rare phenomenon in ancient MSS) has of necessity no such signification. And even if it does sometimes indicate that all the verses which follow are suspicious (of which, however, I have never seen an example), it clearly could not have that signification here, for a reason which I should have thought an intelligent boy might discover.

Well aware, however, that I should never be listened to, with Birch and Griesbach, Scholz and Tischendorf, and indeed every one else against me, I got a learned friend at Rome to visit the Vatican Library for me and inspect the two codices in question. That he would find Birch right in his facts I had no reason to doubt, but I much more than doubted the correctness of his proposed inference from them. I even felt convinced that the meaning and purpose of the asterisks in question would be demonstrably different from what Birch had imagined.

Altogether unprepared was I for the result. It is found that the learned Dane has here made one of those (venial, but) unfortunate blunders to which everyone is liable who registers phenomena of this class in haste and does not methodize these memoranda until he gets home. To be brief, there proves to be no asterisk at all, either in Codex 756 or in Codex 757.

The evidence, therefore, not only breaks hopelessly down; but it is discovered that this witness has been by accident put into the wrong box. This is, in fact, a witness not for the plaintiff but for the defendant! As for the other codex, it exhibits neither asterisk nor cross, but contains the same note or scholion attesting the genuineness of the last twelve verses of St. Mark.

In Codices 20 and 300 (Scholz proceeds) we read as follows: "From here to the end forms no part of the text in some of the copies. In the ancient copies, however, it all forms part of the text." Scholz (who was the first to adduce this important testimony to the genuineness of the verses now under consideration) takes no notice of the singular circumstance that the two MSS he mentions have been exactly assimilated in ancient times to a common model and that they correspond one with the other so entirely that the foregoing rubrical annotation appears in the wrong place in both of them—namely, at the close of verse 15, where it interrupts the text.

This was, therefore, once a scholion written in the margin of some very ancient codex, which has lost its way in the process of transcription (for there can be no doubt that it was originally written against verse 8). And let it be noted that its testimony is express, and that it avouches for the fact that "in the ancient copies" St. Mark 16:9-20 "formed part of the text."

Yet more important is the record contained in the same two MSS (of which also Scholz says nothing), namely, that they exhibit a text which had been "collated with the ancient and approved copies at Jerusalem." What need is there to point out that so remarkable a statement—taken in conjunction with the express voucher that "although some copies of the Gospels are without the verses under discussion, yet that in the ancient copies all the verses are found"—is a critical attestation to the genuineness of St. Mark 16:9-20 far outweighing the bare statement (next to be noticed) of the undeniable historical fact that "in some copies" St. Mark ends at verse 8 but "in many does not"?

But when the twenty MSS which remain undisposed of have been scrutinized, their testimony is found to be quite different from what is commonly supposed. One of them (No. 38) has been cited in error, while the remaining nineteen are nothing else but copies of Victor of Antioch's commentary on St. Mark—no less than sixteen of which contain the famous attestation that in most of the accurate copies, and in particular the authentic Palestinian Codex, the last twelve verses of St. Mark's Gospel were found. And this exhausts the evidence.

So far, therefore, as notes and scholia in MSS are concerned, the sum of the matter proves to be simply this: nine codices are observed to contain a note to the effect that the end of St. Mark's Gospel, though wanting "in some," was yet found "in others," "in many," "in the ancient copies."

Next, four codices contain subscriptions vouching for the genuineness of this portion of the Gospel by declaring that those four codices had been collated with approved copies preserved at Jerusalem.

Lastly, sixteen codices (to which, besides that already mentioned by Scholz, I am able to add at least five others, making twenty-two in all) contain a weighty critical scholion asserting categorically that in "very many" and "accurate copies," specially in the "true Palestinian exemplar," these verses had been found by one who seems to have verified the fact of their existence there for himself.

And now, shall I be thought unfair if, on a review of the

premises. I assert that I do not see a shadow of reason for the imposing statement which has been adopted by Tischendorf, Tregelles, and the rest, that "there exist about thirty codices which state that from the more ancient and more accurate copies of the Gospel, the last twelve verses of St. Mark were absent"?

I repeat, there is not so much as one single codex which contains such a scholion, while twenty-four of those commonly enumerated state the exact reverse. We may now advance a step; but the candid reader is invited to admit that hitherto the supposed hostile evidence is on the contrary entirely in favor of the verses under discussion. ("I called these to curse mine enemies, and, behold, thou hast altogether blessed them these three times.")

Nothing has yet been said about Codex L. This is the designation of an uncial MS of the eighth or the ninth century in the library at Paris. It is chiefly remarkable for the correspondence of its readings with those of Codex B and with certain of the citations in Origen, a peculiarity which recommends Codex L (as it recommends three cursive codices of the Gospels—1, 33, 69,) to the special favor of a school with which whatever is found in Codex B is necessarily right.

It is described as the work of an ignorant foreign copyist, who probably wrote with several MSS before him, but who is found to have been wholly incompetent to determine which reading to adopt and which to reject. Certain it is that he interrupts himself, at the end of verse 8, to write as follows:

"Something to this effect
is also met with:

"All that was commanded them they immediately rehearsed unto Peter and the rest. And after things, from East even unto West, did Jesus Himself send forth by their means the holy and incorruptible message of eternal Salvation."

"But this also is met with after
the words, 'For they were afraid':

"Now, when He was risen early, the first day of the week," &c.

It cannot be needful that I should delay the reader with

any remarks on such a termination of the Gospel as the foregoing. It was evidently the production of someone who desired to remedy the conspicuous incompleteness of his own copy of St. Mark's Gospel, but who had imbibed so little of the spirit of the evangelical narrative that he could not in the least imitate the Evangelist's manner.

As for the scribe who executed Codex L, he was evidently incapable of distinguishing the grossest fabrication from the genuine text. The same worthless supplement is found in the margin of the Harklean Syriac (A.D. 616) and in a few other quarters of less importance.

I pass on, with the single remark that I am utterly at a loss to understand on what principle Codex L—a solitary MS of the eighth or ninth century which exhibits an exceedingly vicious text—is to be thought entitled to so much respectful attention on the present occasion, rebuked as it is for the fallacious evidence it bears concerning the last twelve verses of the second Gospel by all the seventeen remaining uncials (three of which are from three to four years more ancient than itself) and by every cursive copy of the Gospels in existence.

Quite certain at least is it that not the faintest additional probability is established by Codex L that St. Mark's Gospel when it left the hands of its inspired Author was in a mutilated condition. The copyist shows that he was as well acquainted as his neighbors with our actual concluding verses. At the same time he betrays his own incapacity by seeming to view with equal favor the worthless alternative which he deliberately transcribes as well, and to which he gives the foremost place. Not St. Mark's Gospel, but Codex L is the sufferer by this appeal.

Internal Evidence Demonstrated to Be the Very Reverse of Unfavorable to These Verses

A distinct class of objections remains to be considered. An argument much relied on by those who deny or doubt the genuineness of this portion of St. Mark's Gospel is derived from considerations of internal evidence. In the judgment of a recent editor of the New Testament, these twelve verses "bear traces of another hand from that which has shaped the diction and construction of the rest of the Gospel."

They are therefore "an addition to the narrative," of

which "the internal evidence will be found to preponderate vastly against the authorship of Mark." "A difference," says Tregelles, "has been remarked, and truly remarked, between the phraseology of this section and the rest of this Gospel." According to Dr. Davidson, "The phraseology and style of the section are unfavorable to its authenticity." "The characteristic peculiarities which pervade Mark's Gospel do not appear in it; but, on the contrary, terms and expressions . . . phrases and words, are introduced which Mark never uses or terms for which he employs others," states Meyer.

"With verse 9, (says Professor Norton) we suddenly come upon an excerpting process totally different from the previous mode of narration. The passage contains none of Mark's peculiarities (no *eutheos,* no *palin,* etc., but the baldness and lack of clearness which mark a compiler), while in single expressions it is altogether contrary to Mark's manner. . . . There is a difference so great between the use of language in this passage and its use in the undisputed portion of Mark's Gospel, as to furnish strong reasons for believing the passage not genuine."

"No one, however, has expressed himself more strongly on this subject than Tischendorf. . . . *Singula* (continues Norton) *multifariam a Marci ratione abhorrent."* Here, then, is something very like a consensus of hostile opinion, although the terms of the indictment are somewhat vague: difference of "diction and construction"; difference of "phraseology and style"; difference of "terms and expressions"; difference of "words and phrases"; the absence of St. Mark's "characteristic peculiarities."

I suppose, however, that all may be brought under two heads, style and phraseology: meaning by "style" whatever belongs to the Evangelist's manner and by "phraseology" whatever remains. Therefore, we now examine the proofs by which it is proposed to substantiate these confident assertions, and ascertain exactly what they are worth by constant appeals to the Gospel. Throughout this inquiry, we have to do not with opinion but with fact. The unsupported dicta of critics, however distinguished, are entitled to no manner of attention.

In the meantime, as might have been expected, these confident and often repeated asseverations have been by no means unproductive of mischievous results:

> Like ceaseless droppings, which at last are known
> To leave their dint upon the solid stone.

I observe that scholars and divines of the best type (as the Rev. T. S. Green) at last put up with them. The wisest, however, reproduce them under protest and with apology. The names of Tischendorf and Tregelles, Meyer and Davidson command attention. It seems to be thought incredible that they can all be entirely in the wrong. They impose on learned and unlearned readers alike.

"Even Barnabas has been carried away with their dissimulation." He has (to my surprise and regret) two suggestions. The first one is that this entire section of the second Gospel may possibly have been written long after the rest, and that therefore its verbal peculiarities need not perplex or trouble us. It was, I suppose (according to this learned and pious writer), a kind of afterthought, or supplement, or appendix to St. Mark's Gospel. In this way I have seen the last chapter of St. John once and again accounted for.

To which it ought to be a sufficient answer to point out that there is no appearance whatever of any such interval having been interposed between St. Mark 16:8 and 9; that it is highly improbable that any such interval occurred; and that until the "verbal peculiarities" have been ascertained to exist, it is, to say the least, a gratuitous exercise of the inventive faculty to discover reasons for their existence.

Whether there be not something radically unsound and wrong in all such conjectures about "afterthoughts," "supplements," "appendices," and "second editions" when the everlasting Gospel of Jesus Christ is the thing spoken of—a confusing of things heavenly with things earthly which must make the angels weep—I forebear to press on the present occasion.

His other suggestion is that this portion may not have been penned by St. Mark himself after all. By which he clearly means no more than this, that as we are content not to know who wrote the conclusion of the Books of Deuteronomy and Joshua, so, if needful, we may well be content not to know who wrote the end of the Gospel of St. Mark. In reply, I have but to say that after cause has been shown why we should indeed believe that not St. Mark but someone else wrote the end of St. Mark's Gospel, we shall be perfectly willing to acquiesce in the new fact— but not till then.

It is true indeed that here and there a voice has been lifted up in the way of protest against the proposed inference from the familiar premises (for the self-same statements have now been so often reproduced that the eye grows weary at last of the ever-recurring string of offending vocables); but, with one honorable exception, men do not seem to have ever thought of calling the premises themselves in question: examining the statements one by one, contesting the ground inch by inch, refusing absolutely to submit to any dictation whatever in this behalf, insisting on bringing the whole matter to the test of severe inquiry, and making every detail the subject of strict judicial investigation.

This is what I propose to do in the course of the present section. I altogether deny the validity of the inference which has been drawn from "the style," "the phraseology," "the diction" of the present section of the Gospel. But I do more. I entirely deny the accuracy of almost every individual statement from which the unfavorable induction is made and the hostile inference drawn. Even this will not nearly satisfy me. I insist that only one result can attend the exact analysis of this portion of the Gospel into its elements, namely, a profound conviction that St. Mark is most certainly its author.

Let me, however, distinctly declare beforehand that remarks on "the style" of an Evangelist are singularly apt to be fallacious, especially when (as here) it is proposed to apply them to a very limited portion of the sacred narrative.

Altogether to be mistrusted, moreover, are they, when (as on the present occasion) it is proposed to make them the ground for possibly rejecting such a portion of Scripture as spurious. It becomes a fatal objection to such reasoning that the style may indeed be exceedingly diverse and yet the author be confessedly one and the same. How exceedingly dissimilar in style are the Revelation of St. John and the Gospel of St. John!

Moreover, practically, the promised remarks on "style" when the authorship of some portion of Scripture is to be discussed are commonly observed to degenerate at once into what is really quite a different thing. Single words, perhaps some short phrase, is appealed to, which (it is said) does not recur in any part of the same book; and thence it is argued that the author can no longer be the same.

"According to this argument, the recurrence of the same words constitutes identity of style; difference of style in such a sense as compels us to infer diversity of authorship. Each writer is supposed to have at his disposal a limited number of 'formulae' within the range of which he must work. He must in each chapter employ these formulae, and these only. He must be content with one small portion of his mother tongue and not dare to venture across the limits of that portion, on pain of losing his identity" (Dr. Kay).

It scarcely requires illustration to show how utterly insecure must be every approximation to such a method of judging about the authorship of any twelve verses of Scripture which can be named. The attentive reader of St. Matthew's Gospel is aware that a mode of expression which is six times repeated in his eighth and ninth chapters is perhaps only once met with besides in his Gospel, namely, in his twenty-first chapter. The "style" of the seventeenth verse of his first chapter may be thought unlike anything else in St. Matthew.

St. Luke's five opening verses are unique, both in respect of manner and of matter. St. John also in his five opening verses seems to me to have adopted a method which is not recognizable anywhere else in his writings; "rising strangely by degrees," as Bishop Pearson expresses it, "making the last word of the former sentence the first of that which followeth." "He knoweth that he saith true" is the language of the same Evangelist concerning himself in chapter 19:35. But, "we know that his testimony is true" is his phrase in chapter 21:24. Twice, and twice only throughout his Gospel (viz., in chap. 19:35 and 20:31), is he observed to address his readers, and on both occasions in the same words ("that ye may believe").

But what of all this? Is it to be supposed that St. Matthew, St. Luke, St. John are not the authors of those several places? From facts like these no inference whatever is to be drawn as to the genuineness or the spuriousness of a writing. It is quite to mistake the critic's vocation to imagine that he is qualified, or called on, to pass any judgment of the sort.

I have not said all this, of course, as declining the proposed investigation. I approach it, on the contrary, right willingly, being confident that it can be attended by only one result. With what is true, endless are the harmonies which evolve themselves; from what is false, the true is equally certain to stand out divergent. And we all desire nothing but the truth.

To begin, then, with the "style and manner" of St. Mark in this place.

We are assured that "instead of the graphic, detailed description by which this Evangelist is distinguished, we meet with an abrupt, sententious manner, resembling that of brief notices extracted from larger accounts and loosely linked together."

Surely if this be so, the only lawful inference would be that St. Mark, in this place, has "extracted brief notices from larger accounts and loosely linked them together"; and unless such a proceeding on the part of the Evangelist be judged incredible, it is hard to see what is the force of the adverse criticism as directed against the genuineness of the passage now under consideration.

But in truth (when divested of what is merely a gratuitous assumption), the preceding account of the matter is probably not far from the correct one. Of St. Mark's practice of making "extracts" I know nothing—nor Dr. Davidson either. That there existed any "larger accounts" which would have been available for such a purpose (except the Gospel according to St. Matthew), there is neither a particle of evidence nor a shadow of probability.

On the other hand, it is simply undeniable that, notwithstanding the abundant oral information to which confessedly he had access, St. Mark has been Divinely guided in this place to handle, in the briefest manner, some of the chiefest things which took place after our Lord's resurrection. And without at all admitting that the style of the Evangelist is in consequence either "abrupt" or "sententious," I yet recognize the inevitable consequence of relating many dissimilar things within very narrow limits; namely, that the transition from one to the other forces itself on the attention. What wonder that the same phenomenon should not be discoverable in other parts of the Gospel where the Evangelist is not observed to be doing the same thing?

But wherever in his Gospel St. Mark is doing the same thing, he is observed to adopt the style and manner which Dr. Davidson is pleased to call "sententious" and "abrupt." Take twelve verses in his first chapter as an example. Between St. Mark 16:9-20 and St. Mark 1:9-20, I proceed to transcribe the passage which I deliberately propose for comparison—the twelve corresponding verses, namely, in St. Mark's first chapter, which are to be compared with the twelve verses already under discussion from his last chapter; and they may be just as conveniently exhibited in English as in Greek:

St. Mark 1:9-20

(9) And it came to pass in those days, that Jesus came from Nazareth of Galilee, and was baptized of John in Jordan. (10) And straightway coming up out of the water, he saw the heavens opened, and the Spirit like a dove descending upon him: (11) and there came a voice from heaven saying, Thou art my beloved Son, in whom I am well pleased. (12) And immediately the Spirit driveth him into the wilderness. (13) And He was there in the wilderness forty days, tempted of Satan; and was with the wild beasts; and the angels ministered unto him. (14) Now after that John was put in prison, Jesus came into Galilee, preaching the gospel of the kingdom of God, (15) and saying, The time is fulfilled, and the kingdom of God is at hand: repent ye, and believe the gospel. (16) Now, as he walked by the sea of Galilee, he saw Simon and Andrew his brother casting a net into the sea: for they were fishers. (17) And Jesus said unto them, Come ye after me, and I will make you to become fishers of men. (18) And straightway they forsook their nets, and followed him. (19) And when he had gone a little farther thence, he saw James the son of Zebedee, and John his brother, who also were in the ship mending their nets. (20) And straightway he called them; and they left their father Zebedee in the ship with the hired servants, and went after him.

The candid reader must admit that precisely the self-same manner is recognizable in this first chapter of St. Mark's Gospel which is asserted to be peculiar to the last. Note, that from our Savior's baptism (which occupies the first three verses) the Evangelist passes to His temptation, which is dismissed in two verses. Six months elapse. The commencement of the ministry is dismissed in the next two verses. The last five describe the call of four of the apostles, without any distinct allusion to the miracle which was the occasion of it.

How was it possible that when incidents considerable as these had to be condensed within the narrow compass of twelve verses, the same "graphic detailed description" could reappear which renders St. Mark's description of the miracle performed in the country of the Gadarenes (for example) so very interesting; where a single incident is spread over twenty verses, although the action did not perhaps occupy an hour? I rejoice to observe that "the abrupt transitions of this section" (vv. 1-13) have also been noticed by Dean Alford, who very justly accounts for the phenomenon by pointing out that here "Mark appears as an abridger of previously well-known facts." But then I want to know what there is in this to induce us to suspect the genuineness of either the beginning or the end of St. Mark's Gospel?

For it is a mistake to speak as if "graphic, detailed description" invariably characterize the second Gospel. St. Mark is quite as remarkable for his practice of occasionally exhibiting a considerable transaction in a highly abridged form. The opening of his Gospel is singularly concise and altogether sudden.

His account of John's preaching (1:1-8) is the shortest of all. Very concise is his account of our Savior's baptism (vv. 9-11). The brevity of his description of our Lord's temptation is even extraordinary (vv. 12, 13). I pass on, premising that I shall have occasion to remind the reader by and by of certain peculiarities in these same twelve verses that seem to have been hitherto generally overlooked.

Nothing more true, therefore, than Dr. Tregelles' admission "that arguments on style are often very fallacious, and that by themselves they prove very little. But," he proceeds, "when there does exist external evidence; and when internal proofs as to style, manner, verbal expression, and connection are in accordance with such independent grounds of forming a judgment; then, these internal considerations possess very great weight."

I have already shown that there exists no such external evidence as Dr. Tregelles supposes. And in the absence of it, I am bold to assert that since nothing in the "style" or the "phraseology" of these verses ever aroused suspicion in times past, we have rather to be on our guard against suffering our judgment to be warped by arguments drawn from such precarious considerations now.

As for determining from such data the authorship of an isolated passage—asserting or denying its genuineness for no other reason but because it contains certain words and expressions which do or do not occur elsewhere in the Gospel of which it forms a part—let me again declare plainly that the proceeding is in the highest degree uncritical. We are not competent judges of what words an Evangelist was likely on any given occasion to employ. We have no positive knowledge of the circumstances under which any part of any one of the four Gospels was written, nor the influences which determined an Evangelist's choice of certain expressions in preference to others.

As for *ho Kurios* being "foreign to the diction of Mark in speaking of the Lord," I really do not know what the learned critic can possibly mean, unless it is that he finds our Lord nowhere called *ho Kurios* by St. Mark, except in this place.

But, then, he is respectfully reminded that neither does he find our Lord anywhere called "Jesus Christ" by St. Mark, except in chapter 1:1. Are we, therefore, to suspect the beginning of St. Mark's Gospel as well as the end of it? By no means (I shall perhaps be told); a reason is assignable for the use of that expression in chapter 1:1. And so, I venture to reply, there is a fully sufficient reason assignable for the use of this expression in chapter 16:19.

By St. Matthew, by St. Mark, and by St. John our Lord is called *Iēsous Christos*, but only in the first chapter of their respective Gospels. By St. Luke nowhere. The appellation may, or may not, be thought "foreign to the diction" of those Evangelists. But surely it constitutes no reason whatever why we should suspect the genuineness of the beginning of the first, or the second, or the fourth Gospel.

St. John three times in the first verse of his first chapter designates the Eternal Son by the extraordinary title *ho Logos;* but nowhere else in his Gospel (except once in v. 14) does that name recur. Would it be reasonable to represent this as a suspicious circumstance? Is not the Divine fitness of that sublime appellation generally recognized and admitted? Surely, we come to Scripture to be learners only: not to teach the blessed writers how they ought to have spoken about God! When will men learn that "the Scripture phrase, or language of the Holy Ghost" is as much above them as heaven is above earth?

For, after all, the only question to be asked is, will any one pretend that such a circumstance as this is suspicious? Unless that be asserted, I see not what is gained by raking together (as one easily might do in any section of any of the Gospels) every minute peculiarity of form or expression which can possibly be found within the space of these twelve verses.

It is an evidence of nothing so much as an incorrigible coarseness of critical fiber that every slight variety of manner or language should be thus pounced on and represented as a note of spuriousness, in the face of (a) the unfaltering tradition of the Church universal that the document has never been hitherto suspected; and (b) the known proclivity of all writers, as free moral and intellectual agents, sometimes to deviate from their else invariable practice. May I not here close the discussion?

There will perhaps be some who remark that however successfully the foregoing objections may seem to have been severally disposed of, yet the combined force of such a multitude of slightly suspicious circumstances must be not only appreciable, but even remain an inconvenient, not to say a formidable fact. Let me point out that the supposed remark is nothing else but a fallacy which is detected the instant it is steadily looked at. For if there really had remained after the discussion of each of the foregoing twenty-five articles a slight residuum of suspiciousness, then of course the aggregate of so many fractions would have amounted to something in the end.

But since it has been proved that there is absolutely nothing at all suspicious in any of the alleged circumstances which have been examined, the case becomes altogether different. The sum of ten thousand nothings is still nothing.

But enough of all this. Here, we may with advantage review the progress made in this inquiry.

I claim to have demonstrated long since that all those imposing assertions respecting the "style" and "phraseology" of this section of the Gospel which were rehearsed at the outset, are destitute of foundation. But from this discovery alone there results a settled conviction which it will be found difficult henceforth to disturb. A page of Scripture which has been able to endure so severe an ordeal of hostile inquiry has been proved to be above suspicion. That character is rightly accounted blameless which comes out unsullied after calumny has done her worst, done it systematically, done it with a will, done it for a hundred years.

But this is not an adequate statement of the facts of the case in respect of the conclusion of St. Mark's Gospel. Something more is certain than that the charges which have been so industriously brought against this portion of the Gospel are without foundation. It has been also proved that instead of there being discovered twenty-seven suspicious words and phrases scattered up and down these twelve verses of the Gospel, there actually exist exactly as many words and phrases which attest with more or less certainty that those verses are nothing else but the work of the Evangelist.

And now it is high time to explain that though I have hitherto condescended to adopt the method of my opponents, I have done so only in order to show that it proves fatal to themselves. I am, to say the truth, ashamed of what has last been written, so untrustworthy do I deem the method which (following the example of those who have preceded me in this inquiry) I have pursued.

The "concordance test" (for that is probably as apt and intelligible a designation as can be devised for the purely mechanical process whereby it is proposed by a certain school of critics to judge of the authorship of Scripture) is about the coarsest as well as about the most delusive that could be devised. By means of this clumsy and vulgar instrument—expecially when applied (as in the case before us) without skill and discrimination—it would be just as easy to prove that the first twelve verses of St. Mark's Gospel are of a suspicious character as the last. In truth, except in very skillful hands, it is no test at all and can only mislead.

Turning away from all this (not, however, without an apology for having lingered over such frivolous details so long), I desire to point out that we have reverently to look below the surface if we would ascertain how far it is to be presumed from internal considerations whether St. Mark was, or was not, indeed the author of this portion of his Gospel.

We must devise, I say, some more delicate, more philosophical, more real test than the coarse, uncritical expedient which has been hitherto considered of ascertaining by reference to the pages of a Greek concordance whether a certain word which is found in this section of the Gospel is, or is not, used elsewhere by St. Mark. And I suppose it will be generally allowed to be deserving of attention—in fact, to be a singularly corroborative circumstance—that within the narrow compass of these twelve verses we meet with every principal characteristic of St. Mark's manner. Let us examine these.

Though he is the author of the shortest of the Gospels, and though to all appearance he often merely reproduced what St. Matthew had said before him or else anticipates something which is afterward delivered by St. Luke, it is surprising how often we are indebted to St. Mark for precious pieces of information which we look for in vain elsewhere. Now, this is a feature of the Evangelist's manner which is susceptible of memorable illustration from the section before us.

How many and how considerable are the new circumstances which St. Mark here delivers! (1) Mary Magdalene was the first to behold the risen Savior; (2) it was He who had cast out from her the "seven devils"; (3) how the men were engaged to whom she brought her joyful message; (4) these same men not only did not believe her story, but when Cleopas and his companion declared what had happened to themselves, "neither believed they them"; (5) the terms of the Ministerial Commission, as set down in verses 15 and 16, are unique; (6) the announcement of the "signs which should follow them that believe" is even extraordinary; (7) this is the only place in the Gospel where the session at the right hand of God is recorded.

So many and such precious incidents, showered into the Gospel treasury at the last moment and with such a lavish hand, must needs have proceeded if not from an apostle at least from a companion of apostles. Oh, if we had no other token to go by, there could not be a reasonable doubt that this entire section is by no other than St. Mark himself!

A second striking characteristic of the second Evangelist is his love of picturesque, or at least striking details—his proneness to introduce exceedingly minute particulars, often of the profoundest significance and always of considerable interest. Not to look beyond the twelve verses (chapter 1:9-20) which were originally proposed for comparison, we are reminded that in describing our Savior's baptism it is only St. Mark who relates that "he came from Nazareth" to be baptized. In his highly elliptical account of our Lord's temptation, it is only he who relates that "he was with the wild beasts."

In his description of the call of the four disciples, St. Mark alone (notwithstanding the close resemblance of his account to what is found in St. Matthew) records that the father of St. James and St. John was left "in the ship with the hired servants."

St. Mark is observed to introduce many expressions into his Gospel which confirm the prevalent tradition that it was at Rome he wrote it and that it was with an immediate view to Latin readers that it was published. Twelve such expressions were enumerated above and such, it was also there shown, most unmistakably is the phrase *prōtē sabbaton* in verse 9.

It is simply incredible that anyone but an Evangelist writing under the peculiar conditions traditionally assigned to St. Mark would have hit on such an expression as this— the strict equivalent, to Latin ears, for *hē mia sabbatōn* which has occurred just above, in verse 2. Now this, it will be remembered, is one of the hackneyed objections to the genuineness of this entire portion of the Gospel. This is quite proof enough (if proof were needed) of the exceeding improbability which attaches to the phrase, in the judgment of those who have most deeply considered this question.

The last peculiarity of St. Mark to which I propose to invite attention is supplied by those expressions which connect his Gospel with St. Peter, reminding us of the constant traditional belief of the ancient Church that St. Mark was companion of the chief of the apostles.

But besides, and over and above such considerations as those which precede, (some of which, I am aware, might be considerably evacuated of their cogency; while others, I am just as firmly convinced, will remain forcible witnesses of God's truth to the end of time), I hesitate not to avow my personal conviction that abundant and striking evidence is garnered up within the brief compass of these twelve verses that they are identical in respect of fabric with the rest of the Gospel, were clearly manufactured out of the same Divine materials, and were wrought on the same heavenly loom.

It was even to have been expected, from what is found to have been universally the method in other parts of Scripture (for it was of course foreseen by Almighty God from the beginning that this portion of His Word would be, like its Divine Author, in these last days caviled at, reviled, hated, rejected, denied), that the Spirit would not leave Himself without witness in this place.

It was to have been anticipated, I say, that Eternal Wisdom would carefully (I trust there is no irreverence in so speaking of God and His ways!) make provision: meet the coming unbelief (as His Angel met Balaam) with a drawn sword; plant up and down throughout these twelve verses of the Gospel sure indications of their Divine original—unmistakable notes of purpose and design, mysterious traces and tokens of Himself; not visible indeed to the scornful and arrogant, the impatient and irreverent; yet clear as if written with a sunbeam to the patient and humble student, the man who "trembleth at God's Word."

Or (if the reader prefers the image) the indications of a Divine original to be met with in these verses will be likened rather to those cryptic characters, invisible so long as they remain unsuspected but which shine forth clear and strong when exposed to the light or to the heat (light and heat, both emblems of Himself!), so that even he that gropeth in darkness must now see them and admit that of a truth "the Lord is in this place" although he "knew it not"!

When I scrutinize attentively the two portions of Scripture thus proposed for critical survey, I am not a little struck by the discovery that the Sixth Article of the ancient Creed of Jerusalem (A.D. 348) is found in the one and the Fifth Article, in the other. If it be a purely fortuitous circumstance that two cardinal verities like these (viz., "He ascended into heaven, and sat down at the right hand of God,"—and "One baptism for the remission of sins") should be found at either extremity of one short

Gospel, I will but point out that it is certainly one of a very remarkable series of fortuitous circumstances. But in the thing to be mentioned next, there neither is, nor can be, any talk of fortuitousness at all.

Allusion is made to the diversity of names whereby the Son of Man is indicated in these two places of the Gospel, which constitutes a most Divine circumstance and is profoundly significant. He who in the first verse (St. Mark 1:1) was designated by the joint title *"Iēsous"* and *"Christos,"* in the last two verses (St. Mark 16:19, 20) is styled for the first and for the last time *"Ho Kurios"*—the Lord.

And why? Because He who at His circumcision was named "Jesus" (a name which was given Him from His birth, yea, and before His birth), He who at His baptism became "the Christ" (a title which belonged to His office, and which betokens His sacred unction)—the same, on the occasion of His ascension into heaven and session at the right hand of God, when (as we know) "all power had been given unto him in heaven and in earth" (St. Matt. 28:18)—is designated by His name of dominion: "the Lord" Jehovah. . . . *"Magnifica et opportuna appellatio!"*, as Bengel well remarks.

But I take leave to point out that all this never would or could have entered into the mind of a fabricator of a conclusion to St. Mark's unfinished Gospel. No inventor of a supplement, I say, could have planted his foot in this way in exactly the right place. The proof of my assertion is because the present indication that the Holy Ghost was indeed the author of these last twelve verses is even appealed to by Dr. Davidson and his school as a proof of a spurious original. Verily, such critics do not recognize the token of the Divine finger even when they see it!

It is an extraordinary note of genuineness that such a vast number of minute but important facts should be found accumulated within the narrow compass of these twelve verses, and should be met with nowhere else. The writer (supposing that he had only St. Matthew's Gospel before him) traverses—except in one single instance—wholly new ground, moving forward with unmistakable boldness and a rare sense of security. Wherever he plants his foot, it is to enrich the soil with fertility and beauty.

But on the supposition that he wrote after St. Luke's

and St. John's Gospels had appeared, the marvel becomes increased a hundredfold. For example, how then does it come to pass that he evidently draws his information from quite independent sources, is not bound by any of their statements, and even seems purposely to break away from their guidance and to adventure some extraordinary statement of his own—which nevertheless carries the true Gospel savor with it and is felt to be authentic from the very circumstance that no one would have ever dared to invent such a detail and put it forth on his own responsibility?

What would be gained by demonstrating (as I am of course prepared to do) that there is really no inconsistency whatever between anything St. Mark here says and what the other Evangelists deliver? I should have proved that (assuming the other evangelical narratives to be authentic, i.e., historically true) the narrative before us cannot be objected to on the score of its not being authentic also. But by whom is such proof required? Not by the men who insist that errors are occasionally to be met with in the evangelical narratives. In their estimation, the genuineness of an inspired writing is a thing not in the least degree rendered suspicious by the erroneousness of its statements. According to them, the narrative may exhibit inaccuracies and inconsistencies, and may yet be the work of St. Mark.

If the inconsistencies be but "trifling" and the inaccuracies "minute," these "sound theologians" (for so they style themselves) "have no dread whatever of acknowledging" their existence. Be it so. Then would it be a gratuitous task to set about convincing them that no inconsistency, no inaccuracy is discoverable within the compass of these twelve concluding verses.

But neither is such proof required by faithful readers who, for want of the requisite scientific knowledge, are unable to discern the perfect harmony of the evangelical narratives in this place. It is only one of many places where a prima facie discrepancy, though it does not fail to strike, yet (happily) altogether fails to distress them.

Consciously or unconsciously, such readers reason with themselves somewhat as follows: "God's Word, like all God's other works (and I am taught to regard God's Word as a very masterpiece of creative skill), the blessed Gospel, I say, is full of difficulties. And yet those difficulties are observed invariably to disappear under competent investigation.

"Can I seriously doubt that if sufficient critical skill were brought to bear on the highly elliptical portion of narrative contained in these twelve verses, it would present no exception to a rule which is observed to be else universal; and that any apparent inconsistency between St. Mark's statements in this place, and those of St. Luke and St. John, would also be found to be imaginary only?"

Let it suffice that, in the foregoing pages—

1. I have shown that the supposed argument from "style" (in itself a highly fallacious test) disappears under investigation.

2. It has been proved that, on the contrary, the style of St. Mark 16:9-20 is exceedingly like the style of St. Mark 1:9-20; and therefore, that it is rendered probable by the style that the author of the beginning of this Gospel was also the author of the end of it.

3. I have ·further shown that the supposed argument from "phraseology" (in itself, a most unsatisfactory test; and as it has been applied to the matter in hand, a very coarse and clumsy one) breaks down hopelessly under severe analysis.

4. Instead of there being twenty-seven suspicious circumstances in the phraseology of these twelve verses, it has been proved that in twenty-seven particulars there emerge corroborative considerations.

5. I have shown that a loftier method of criticism is at hand; and that, tested by this truer, more judicious, and more philosophical standard, a presumption of the highest order is created that these verses must needs be the work of St. Mark.

The Testimony of
the Lectionaries Shown to Be Absolutely Decisive
as to the Genuineness of These Verses

I have reserved for the last the testimony of the Lectionaries, which has been hitherto all but entirely overlooked—passed by without so much as a word of comment by those who have preceded me in this inquiry. Yet it is, when rightly understood, altogether decisive of the question at issue. And why? Because it is not the testimony rendered by a solitary Father or by a solitary MS, nor even the testimony yielded by a single Church, or by a single family of MSS. But it is the united testimony of all the Churches.

It is therefore the evidence borne by a "goodly fellowship of prophets," "a noble army of martyrs" indeed, as well as by MSS innumerable which have long since perished but which must of necessity once have existed. And so, it comes to us like the voice of many waters: dates (as I shall show by and by) from a period of altogether immemorial antiquity; is endorsed by the sanction of all the succeeding ages; admits of neither doubt nor evasion.

This subject, in order that it may be intelligibly handled, will be most conveniently approached by some remarks which will rehearse the matter from the beginning.

The Christian Church succeeded to the Jewish. The younger society inherited the traditions of the elder, not less as a measure of necessity than as a matter of right; and by a kind of sacred instinct conformed itself from the very beginning in countless particulars to its divinely appointed model. The same general order of service went on unbroken, conducted by a priesthood whose spiritual succession was at least as jealously guarded as had been the natural descent from Aaron in the Church of the circumcision.

It was found that "the sacraments of the Jews are [but] types of ours." Still were David's Psalms antiphonally recited, and the voices of "Moses and the Prophets" were heard in the sacred assemblies of God's people "every Sabbath day." Canticle succeeded to canticle, while many a versicle simply held its ground. The congenial utterances of the chosen race passed readily into the service of the family of the redeemed.

Unconsciously perhaps, the very method of the one became adopted by the other; for example, the method of beginning a festival from the "eve" of the preceding holy day. The synagogue worship became transfigured, but it did not part with one of its characteristic features. Above all, the same three great festivals were still retained which declare "the rock whence we are hewn and the hole of the pit whence we are digged"; only it was made a question rather (a controversy) whether Easter should or should not be celebrated with the Jews.

But the reader's attention is now exclusively invited to

the faithful handing on to the Christian community of the Lectionary practice of the synagogue. That the Christian Church inherited from Jewish custom the practice of reading a first and a second Lesson in its public assemblies is demonstrable. What the synagogue practice was in the time of the apostles is known from Acts 8:15, 27. Justin Martyr (A.D. 150) describes the Christian practice in his time as precisely similar: only that for "the Law," there is found to have been at once substituted "the Gospel." He speaks of the writings of "the Apostles" and of "the Prophets."

Chrysostom has the same expression (for the two Lessons) in one of his Homilies. Cassian (A.D. 400) says that in Egypt, after the Twelve Prayers at Vespers and at Matins, two Lessons were read, one out of the Old Testament and the other out of the New. But on Saturdays and Sundays, and the fifty days of Pentecost, both Lessons were from the New Testament—one from the Epistles or the Acts of the Apostles, the other from the Gospels.

Our own actual practice seems to bear a striking resemblance to that of the Christian Church at the earliest period; for we hear of "Moses and the Prophets" (which will have been the carrying on of the old synagogue method, represented by our first and second Lesson), a lesson out of the "Epistles or Acts," together with a lesson out of the "Gospels." It is, in fact, universally received that the Eastern Church has, from a period of even apostolic antiquity, enjoyed a Lectionary—or established system of Scripture lessons—of her own.

In its conception, this Lectionary is discovered to have been fashioned (as was natural) on the model of the Lectionary of God's ancient people, the Jews; for it commences, as theirs did, in the autumn (in September) and prescribes two immovable "Lections" for every Saturday (as well as for every Sunday) in the year. It differs chiefly in this, that the prominent place which had previously been assigned to "the Law and the Prophets" was henceforth enjoyed by the Gospels and the apostolic writings.

That the practice in the Christian Church of reading publicly before the congregation certain fixed portions of Holy Writ, according to an established and generally received rule, must have existed from a period long anterior to the date of any known Greek copy of the New

Testament Scriptures.

That although there happens to be extant neither *"Synaxarium"* (i.e., Table of Proper Lessons of the Greek Church) nor *"Evangelistarium"* (i.e., book containing the Ecclesiastical Lections *in extenso*) of higher antiquity than the eighth century, yet that the scheme itself, as exhibited by those monuments—certainly in every essential particular—is older than any known Greek MS which contains it, by at least four, in fact by full five hundred years.

In the said Lectionaries of the Greek and of the Syrian Churches, the twelve concluding verses of St. Mark which are the subject of discussion throughout the present pages are observed invariably to occupy the same singularly conspicuous as well as most honorable place.

The first of the foregoing propositions is an established fact. It is at least quite certain that in the fourth century (if not long before) there existed a known Lectionary system, alike in the Church of the East and of the West. Cyril of Jerusalem (A.D. 348) speaking about our Lord's ascension, remarks that by a providential coincidence, on the previous day, which was Sunday, the event had formed the subject of the appointed lessons, and that he had availed himself of the occasion to discourse largely on the subject.

Chrysostom, preaching at Antioch, makes it plain that, in the latter part of the fourth century, the order of the lessons which were publicly read in the church on Saturdays and Sundays was familiarly known to the congregation; for he invites them to sit down and study attentively beforehand, at home, the sections of the Gospel which they were about to hear in church. Augustine is express in recording that in his time proper lessons were appointed for festival days, and that an innovation which he had attempted on Good Friday had given general offense.

Now by these few notices, to look no further, it is rendered certain that a lectionary system of some sort must have been in existence at a period long anterior to the date of any extant copy of the New Testament Scriptures.

The Oriental Lectionary consists of *"Synaxarion"* and *"Eclogadion"* (or Tables of Proper Lessons from the Gospels and apostolic writings daily throughout the year), together with *"Menologion"* (or Calendar of immovable

Festivals and Saints' Days). That we are thoroughly
acquainted with all of these, as exhibited in codices of the
eighth, ninth, and tenth centuries, is a familiar fact. . . .
But it is no less certain that the scheme of Proper Lessons
itself is of much higher antiquity.

The proof of this, if it could only be established by an
induction of particular instances, would not only be very
tedious but also very difficult indeed. It will be perceived,
on reflection, that even when the occasion of a homily
(suppose) is actually recorded, the Scripture references
which it contains (apart from the author's statement that
what he quotes had formed part of that day's service)
creates scarcely so much as a presumption of the fact. At
the same time, the correspondence, however striking,
between such references to Scripture and the Lectionary as
we have it, is of course no proof whatever that we are so
far in possession of the Lectionary of the patristic age.
Nay, on famous festivals the employment of certain
passages of Scripture is, in a manner, inevitable and may
on no account be pressed.

Thus, when Chrysostom and when Epiphanius,
preaching on Ascension Day, refer to Acts 1:10, 11, we do
not feel ourselves warranted to press the coincidence of
such a quotation with the liturgical section of the day. So,
again, when Chrysostom preaches on Christmas Day and
quotes from St. Matthew 2:1, 2, or on Whitsunday and
quotes from St. John 7:38 and Acts 2:3 and 13, though
both places form part of the liturgical sections for the day,
no proof results therefrom that either chapter was actually
used.

But we are not reduced to this method. It is discovered
that nearly three-fourths of Chrysostom's Homilies on St.
Matthew either begin at the first verse of a known
ecclesiastical lection or else at the first ensuing verse after
the close of one. Thirteen of those homilies in succession
(the 63rd to the 75th inclusive) begin with the first words
of as many known lections. "Let us attend to this delight-
ful section which we never cease turning to" are the
opening words of Chrysostom's 79th Homily, of which
"the text" is St. Matthew 25:31, that is, the beginning of
the Gospel for Sexagesima Sunday. Cyril of Alexandria's
so-called Commentary on St. Luke is nothing else but a
series of short sermons, for the most part delivered on

known ecclesiastical lections, which does not seem to have been as yet observed. Augustine (A.D. 416) says expressly that he had handled St. John's Gospel in precisely the same way. All of this is significant in a high degree.

I proceed, however, to adduce a few distinct proofs that the existing Lectionary of the great Eastern Church, as it is exhibited by Matthaei, by Scholz, and by Scrivener from MSS of the eighth century and which is contained in Syriac MSS of the sixth and seventh must needs be in the main a work of extraordinary antiquity. And if I do not begin by insisting that at least one century more may be claimed for it by a mere appeal to the Hierosolymitan Version, it is only because I will never knowingly admit what may prove to be untrustworthy materials into my foundations.

"Every one is aware," says Chrysostom in a sermon on our Savior's baptism, preached at Antioch, A.D. 387, "that this is called the Festival of the Epiphany. Two manifestations are thereby intended: concerning both of which you have heard this day St. Paul discourse in his Epistle to Titus."

Then follows a quotation from Titus 2:11-13, which proves to be the beginning of the lection for the day in the Greek Menology. In the time of Chrysostom, therefore, Titus 2:11, 12, 13 formed part of one of the Epiphany lessons, as it does to this hour in the Eastern Church. What is scarcely less interesting, it is also found to have been part of the Epistle for the Epiphany in the old Gallican Liturgy, whose affinities with the East are well known.

Epiphanius (speaking of the feasts of the Church) says that at the nativity a star showed that the Word had become incarnate; at the "Theophania" (our Epiphany) John cried, "Behold the Lamb of God," and so forth, and a voice from heaven proclaimed Him at His baptism. Accordingly, St. Matthew 2:1-12 is found to be the ancient lection for Christmas Day with St. Mark 1:9-11 and St. Matthew 3:13-17 the lections for Epiphany. On the morrow, was read St. John 1:29-34.

In another of his homilies, Chrysostom explains with considerable emphasis the reason why the Book of Acts was read publicly in church during the interval between Easter and Pentecost, remarking that it had been the liturgical arrangement of a yet earlier age.

After such an announcement, it becomes a very striking circumstance that Augustine also (A.D. 412) should be found to bear witness to the prevalence of the same liturgical arrangement in the African Church. In the old Gallican Lectionary, as might have been expected, the same rule is recognizable.

It ought to be needless to add that the same arrangement is observed universally to prevail in the Lectionaries both of the East and of the West to the present hour. This fact, however, must have been lost sight of by the individuals who recently, under pretense of "making some advantageous alterations" in our Lectionary, have constructed an entirely new one, vicious in principle and liable to the gravest objections throughout. Thus this link which bound the Church of England to the practice of primitive Christendom has been unhappily broken and this note of catholicity has been effaced.

The purely arbitrary arrangement (as Mr. Scrivener phrases it) by which the Book of Genesis, instead of the Gospel, is appointed to be read on the week days of Lent, is discovered to have been fully recognized in the time of Chrysostom. Accordingly, the two series of homilies on the Book of Genesis which that Father preached, he preached in Lent.

It will be seen in the next chapter that it was from a very remote period the practice of the Eastern Church to introduce into the lesson for Thursday in holy week, St. Luke's account (chap. 22:43, 44) of our Lord's "agony and bloody sweat" immediately after St. Matthew 26:39. That is, no doubt, the reason why Chrysostom, who has been suspected (I think unreasonably) of employing an Evangelistarium instead of a copy of the Gospels in the preparation of his Homilies, is observed to quote those same two verses in that very place in his Homily on St. Matthew. This shows that the Lectionary system of the Eastern Church in this respect is at least as old as the fourth century.

In conclusion, I may be allowed so far to anticipate what will be found fully established in the next chapter, as to point out here that since in countless places the text of our oldest Evangelia as well as the readings of the primitive Fathers exhibit unmistakable traces of the corrupting influence of the Lectionary practice, that very fact becomes irrefragable evidence of the antiquity of the Lectionary which is the occasion of it.

Not only must it be more ancient than Codex B or Codex Aleph (which are referred to the beginning of the fourth century), but it must be older than Origen in the third century or the Vetus Itala and the Syriac in the second. And thus it is demonstrated, first, that fixed Lessons were read in the churches of the East in the immediately postapostolic age; and, second, that, wherever we are able to test it, the Lectionary of that remote period corresponded with the Lectionary which has come down to us in documents of the sixth century, and was in fact constructed in precisely the same way.

I am content in fact to dismiss the preceding instances with this general remark: a system which is found to have been fully recognized throughout the East and the West in the beginning of the fourth century must of necessity have been established very long before. It is as when we read of three British bishops attending the Council at Arles, A.D. 314. The Church (we say) which could send out those three bishops must have been fully organized at a greatly antecedent period.

Let us attend, however, to the great Festivals of the Church. These are declared by Chrysostom (in a homily delivered at Antioch Dec. 20 A.D. 386) to be the five following: Nativity, the Theophania, Pascha, Ascension, and Pentecost. Epiphanius, his contemporary (Bishop of Constantia in the island of Cyprus), makes the same enumeration in a homily on the ascension. In the Apostolical Constitutions, the same five Festivals are enumerated. Let me state a few liturgical facts in connection with each of these.

It is plain that the preceding enumeration could not have been made at any earlier period, for the Epiphany of our Savior and His Nativity were originally but one Festival. Moreover, the circumstances are well known under which Chrysostom (A.D. 386) announced to his Eastern auditory that in conformity with what had been correctly ascertained at Rome, the ancient Festival was henceforth to be disintegrated. But this is not material to the present inquiry.

We know that, as a matter of fact, "the Epiphanies" became in consequence distributed over December 25 and

January 5. Our Lord's baptism was the event chiefly
commemorated on the latter anniversary, which used to be
observed mainly in honor of His birth. Concerning the
Lessons for Passiontide and Easter, as well as those for the
Nativity and Epiphany, something has been offered already; to which it may be added the Hesychius, in the
opening sentences of that homily which has already
engaged so much of our attention, testifies that the conclusion of St. Mark's Gospel was in his days, as it has been
ever since, one of the lections for Easter. He begins by
saying that the Evangelical narratives of the resurrection
were read on the Sunday night, and proceeds to reconcile
St. Mark's with the rest. Chrysostom once and again
adverts to the practice of discontinuing the reading of the
Acts after Pentecost, which is observed to be also the
method of the Lectionaries.

I speak separately of the Festival of the Ascension, for
an obvious reason. It ranked, as we have seen, in the
estimation of primitive Christendom, with the greatest
Festivals of the Church. Augustine, in a well-known
passage, hints that it may have been of apostolical origin;
so exceedingly remote was its institution accounted in the
days of the great African Father, as well as so entirely
forgotten by that time was its first beginning. I have to
show that in the Great Oriental Lectionary (whether of the
Greek or of the Syrian Church) the last twelve verses of St.
Mark's Gospel occupy a conspicuous as well as a most
honorable place. And this is easily done as the following
will testify.

The Lesson for Matins on Ascension Day in the East, in
the oldest documents to which we have access, consisted
(as now it does) of the last twelve verses—neither more nor
less—of St. Mark's Gospel. At the Liturgy on Ascension St.
Luke 24:36-53 was read; but at Matins, it was St. Mark
16:9-20. The witness of the *"Synaxaria"* is constant to this
effect.

The same lection precisely was adopted among the
Syrians by the Melchite Churches (the party which maintained the decrees of the Council of Chalcedon), and it is
found appointed also in the *Evangelarium Hierosolymitanum.*

In the *Evangelistarium* used in the Jacobite (i.e., the
Monophysite) Churches of Syria, a striking difference of

arrangements is discoverable. While St. Luke 24:36-53 was read at Vespers and at Matins on Ascension Day, the last seven verses of St. Mark's Gospel (chap. 16:14-20) were read at the Liturgy. Strange, that the self-same Gospel should have been adopted at a remote age by some of the Churches of the West, and should survive in our own Book of Common Prayer to this hour!

But St. Mark 16:9-20 was not only appointed by the Greek Church to be read on Ascension Day. Those same twelve verses constitute the third of the eleven "Matin Gospels of the Resurrection," which were universally held in high esteem by the Eastern Churches (Greek and Syrian) and were read successively on Sundays at Matins throughout the year, as well as daily throughout Easter week.

A rubricated copy of St. Mark's Gospel in Syriac, certainly older than A.D. 583, attests that St. Mark 16:9-20 was the "Lection for the great First Day of the Week" (*megalē kuriakē,* i.e., Easter Day). Other copies almost as ancient add that it was used "at the end of the service at the dawn."

Further, these same twelve verses constituted the Lesson at Matins for the second Sunday after Easter, a Sunday which by the Greeks is called *kuriake tōn murophorōn* but with the Syrians bore the names of "Joseph and Nicodemus." So also in the *"Evangelarium Hierosolymitanum."*

Next, in the Monophysite churches of Syria, St. Mark 16:9-18 (or 9-20) was also read at Matins on Easter Tuesday. In the Gallican Church, the third lection for Easter Monday extended from St. Mark 15:47-16:11; for Easter Tuesday, from 16:12 to the end of the Gospel. Augustine says that in Africa also these concluding verses of St. Mark's Gospel used to be publicly read at Eastertide. The same verses (beginning with v. 9) are indicated in the oldest extant Lectionary of the Roman Church.

Lastly, it may be stated that St. Mark 16:9-20 was with the Greeks the Gospel for the Festival of St. Mary Magdalene, July 22.

One knows wondrous little about this department of sacred science who can require to be informed that such a weight of public testimony as this to the last twelve verses of a Gospel is simply overwhelming. The single discovery that in the age of Augustine (385-430) this portion of St. Mark's Gospel was unquestionably read at Easter in the

Churches of Africa, added to the express testimony of the author of the Second Homily on the Resurrection, and of the oldest Syriac MSS, that they were also read by the Orientals at Easter in the public services of the church, must be held to be in a manner decisive of the question.

Let the evidence, then, which is borne by ecclesiastical usage to the genuineness of St. Mark 16:9-20 be summed up, and the entire case caused again to pass under review.

That lessons from the New Testament were publicly read in the assemblies of the faithful according to a definite scheme and on an established system at least as early as the fourth century, has been shown to be a plain historical fact.

Cyril, at Jerusalem (and by implication, his namesake at Alexandria) Chrysostom, at Antioch and at Constantinople, Augustine, in Africa—all four expressly witness to the circumstance. In other words, there is found to have been at least at that time fully established throughout the Churches of Christendom a Lectionary which seems to have been essentially one and the same in the West and in the East. That it must have been of even apostolic antiquity may be inferred from several considerations. But that it dates its beginning from a period anterior to the age of Eusebius, which is the age of Codices B and Aleph, at least admits of no controversy.

Next, documents of the sixth century put us in possession of the great Oriental Lectionary as it is found at that time to have universally prevailed throughout the vast unchanging East. In other words, several of the actual Service Books, in Greek and in Syriac, have survived the accidents of fully a thousand years; and rubricated copies of the Gospels carry us back three centuries further.

The entire agreement which is observed to prevail among these several documents—added to the fact that when they are tested by allusions of fourth century Greek Fathers to what was then the ecclesiastical practice, countless highly significant notes of correspondence emerge—warrants us in believing (in the absence of testimony of any sort to the contrary) that the Lectionary we speak of differs in no essential respect from that system of Lections with which the Church of the fourth century was universally acquainted.

Nothing scarcely is more forcibly impressed on us in the

course of the present inquiry than the fact that documents alone are wanting to make that altogether demonstrable which, in default of such evidence, must remain a matter of inevitable inference only. The forms we are pursuing at last disappear from our sight, but it is only the mist of the early morning which shrouds them. We still hear their voices, still track their footsteps, knowing that others still see them although we ourselves see them no longer. We are sure that they are still there.

Moreover they may yet reappear at any moment. Thus, there exist Syriac MSS of the Gospels of the seventh and even of the sixth century, in which the lessons are rubricated in the text or on the margin. A Syriac MS (of part of the Old Testament) is actually dated A.D. 464. Should an Evangelium of similar date ever come to light of which the rubrication was evidently by the original scribe, the evidence of the Lectionaries would at once be carried back fully three hundred years.

But in fact we stand in need of no such testimony. Acceptable as it would be, it is plain that it would add no strength to the argument whatever. We are already able to plant our footsteps securely in the fourth and even in the third century. It is not enough to insist that inasmuch as the liturgical method of Christendom was at least fully established in the East and in the West at the close of the fourth century, it therefore must have had its beginning at a far remoter period. Our two oldest codices (B and Aleph) bear witness throughout to the corrupting influence of a system which was evidently in full operation before the time of Eusebius.

And even this is not all. The readings in Origen and of the earliest versions of the Gospel (the old Latin, the Syriac, the Egyptian versions) carry back our evidence on this subject unmistakably to the age immediately succeeding that of the apostles. This will be found established in the course of the ensuing chapter.

Beginning our survey of the problem at the opposite end, we arrive at the same result. We have even a deepened conviction that in its essential structure, the Lectionary of the Eastern Church must be of truly primitive antiquity: indeed that many of its leading provisions must date back almost—nay quite—to the apostolic age. From whichever side we approach this question and whatever test we are able to apply to our premises, our conclusion remains still the very same.

Into this Lectionary, then, so universal in its extent, so consistent in its witness, so apostolic in its antiquity, the last twelve verses of the Gospel According to St. Mark from the very first are found to have won for themselves not only an entrance, a lodgment, an established place, but, the place of highest honor—an audience on two of the Church's chiefest festivals.

The circumstance is far too important, far too significant to be passed by without a few words of comment.

For it is not here (be it carefully observed) as when we appeal to some patristic citation, that the recognition of a phrase or a verse or a couple of verses must be accepted as a proof that the same ancient Father recognized the context also in which those words are found. Not so. All the twelve verses in dispute are found in every known copy of the venerable Lectionary of the East. Those same twelve verses—neither more nor less—are observed to constitute one integral lection.

But even this is not all. The most important fact seems to be that to these verses has been assigned a place of the highest possible distinction. It is found that, from the very first, St. Mark 16:9-20 has been everywhere, and by all branches of the Church Catholic, claimed for two of the Church's greatest festivals—Easter and Ascension.

A more weighty or a more significant circumstance can scarcely be imagined. To suppose that a portion of Scripture singled out for such extraordinary honor by the Church universal is a spurious addition to the Gospel is purely irrational and simply monstrous. No unauthorized "fragment," however "remarkable," could by possibility have so established itself from the very first in the regard of the East and the West.

No suspected "addition, placed here in very early times," would have been tolerated in the Church's solemn public service six or seven times a year. No; it is impossible. Had it been one short clause which we were invited to surrender: a verse, two verses, even three or four—the plea being that (as in the case of the celebrated *Pericope de Adultera*) the Lectionaries knew nothing of them—the case would have been entirely different.

But for anyone to seek to persuade us that these twelve

verses, which exactly constitute one of the Church's most famous lections, are every one of them spurious—that the fatal taint begins with the first verse and only ends with the last—this is a demand on our simplicity which, in a less solemn subject, would only provoke a smile. We are constrained.

Have the critics, then (supposing them to be familiar with the evidence which has now been set forth so much in detail), utterly taken leave of their senses? Or do they really suppose that we have taken leave of ours?

It is time to close this discussion. It was declared at the outset that the witness of the Lectionaries to the genuineness of these verses, though it has been generally overlooked, is the most important of any. It admits of no evasion, being simply, as it is, decisive.

I have now fully explained the grounds of that assertion. I have set the verses, which I undertook to vindicate and establish, on a basis from which it will be found impossible any more to dislodge them. Whatever Griesbach, Tischendorf, Tregelles, and the rest may think about the matter, the Holy Eastern Church in her corporate capacity has never been of their opinion. They may doubt. The ante-Nicene Fathers at least never doubted. If the last twelve verses of St. Mark were deservedly omitted from certain copies of his Gospel in the fourth century, it is utterly incredible that these same twelve verses should have been disseminated, by their authority, throughout Christendom; read, by their command, in all the Churches; selected, by their collective judgment, from the whole body of Scripture for the special honor of being listened to once and again at Easter time, as well as on Ascension Day.

The Omission of These Twelve Verses in Certain Ancient Copies of the Gospel Explained and Accounted For

I am much mistaken if the suggestion which I am about to offer has not already presented itself to every reader of ordinary intelligence who has taken the trouble to follow the course of my argument thus far with attention. It requires no acuteness whatever—it is, as it seems to me, the merest instinct of mother wit—on reaching the present stage of the discussion, to debate with oneself somewhat as follows.

So, then, the last twelve verses of St. Mark's Gospel were anciently often observed to be missing from the copies. Eusebius expressly says so. I observe that he nowhere says that their genuineness was anciently suspected. As for himself, his elaborate discussion of their contents convinces me that individually he regarded them with favor. The mere fact (it is best to keep to his actual statement) that "the entire passage" was "not met with in all the copies" is the sum of his evidence; and two extant Greek manuscripts, supposed to be of the fourth century (Codices B and Aleph) mutilated in this precise way, testify to the truth of his statement.

But then it is found that these selfsame twelve verses—neither more nor less—anciently constituted an integral ecclesiastical lection. This lection—inasmuch as it is found to have established itself in every part of Christendom at the earliest period to which liturgical evidence reaches back, and to have been assigned from the very first to two of the chiefest Church festivals—must needs be a lection of almost apostolic antiquity.

Eusebius, I observe, designates the portion of Scripture in dispute by its technical name, *kephalaion* or *perikope* (for so an ecclesiastical lection was anciently called). Here then is a rare coincidence indeed. It is in fact simply unique. Surely, I may add that it is in the highest degree suggestive also. It inevitably provokes the inquiry, Must not these two facts be not only connected but even interdependent?

Will not the omission of the twelve concluding verses from certain ancient copies of Mark's Gospel have been in some way occasioned by the fact that those same twelve verses constituted an integral Church lection? How is it possible to avoid suspecting that the phenomenon to which Eusebius invites attention (viz., that certain copies of St. Mark's Gospel in very ancient times had been mutilated from the end of the 8th verse onwards) ought to be capable of illustration—will have in fact to be explained and in a word accounted for—by the circumstance that at the 8th verse of St. Mark's 16th chapter, one ancient lection came to an end and another ancient lection began?

Somewhat thus (I venture to think) must every unprejudiced reader of intelligence hold parley with himself on reaching the close of the preceding chapter. I need hardly add that I am thoroughly convinced he would be reasoning rightly. I am going to show that the Lectionary practice of the ancient Church does indeed furnish a sufficient clue for the unraveling of this now famous problem. In other words, it enables us satisfactorily to account for the omission of these twelve verses from ancient copies of the collected Gospels.

But I mean to do more. I propose to make my appeal to documents which will be observed to bear no faltering witness in my favor. More yet. I propose that Eusebius himself, the chief author of all this trouble, will be brought back into court and invited to resyllable his evidence. I am much mistaken if even he will not be observed to let fall a hint that we have at last got on the right scent, have accurately divined how this mistake took its beginning, and (what is not least to the purpose) have correctly apprehended what was his own real meaning in what he said.

The proposed solution of the difficulty, if not the evidence on which it immediately rests, might no doubt be exhibited within exceedingly narrow limits. Set down abruptly, however, its weight and value would inevitably fail to be recognized, even by those who already enjoy some familiarity with these studies.

Very few of the considerations which I shall have to rehearse are in fact unknown to critics; yet it is evident that their bearing on the problem before us has hitherto altogether escaped their notice. On the other hand, by one entirely a novice to this department of sacred science, I could scarcely hope to be so much as understood. Let me be allowed, therefore, to preface what I have to say with a few explanatory details which I promise will not be tedious and which I trust will not be found altogether without interest. If they are anywhere else to be met with, it is my misfortune, not my fault, that I have been until now unsuccessful in discovering the place.

From the earliest ages of the Church (as I showed before) it has been customary to read certain definite portions of Holy Scripture, determined by ecclesiastical authority, publicly before the congregation. In process of time, as was natural, the sections so required for public use were collected into separate volumes; lections from the Gospels were written in a book called *"Evangelistarium,"*

and lections from the Acts and Epistles in a book called
"Praxapostolus." These Lectionary books, both Greek and
Syriac, are extant in great numbers, and (I may remark in
passing) deserve a far greater amount of attention than has
been bestowed on them.

It has not been ascertained when the Lectionary first
took the form of a separate book. That no copy is known
to exist (whether in Greek or in Syriac) older than the
eighth century proves nothing. Codices in daily use (like
the Bibles used in our churches) must of necessity have
been of exceptionally brief duration; and Lectionaries,
more even than Biblical MSS, were liable to injury and
decay.

But it is to be observed (and to explain this, is much
more to my present purpose) that besides transcribing the
ecclesiastical lections into separate books, it became the
practice at a very early period to adapt copies of the
Gospels to lectionary purposes. I suspect that this practice
began in the churches of Syria; for Syriac copies of the
Gospels (at least of the seventh century) abound, which
have the lections more or less systematically rubricated in
the text.

There is in the British Museum a copy of St. Mark's
Gospel according to the Peshito version, certainly written
previous to A.D. 583, which has at least five or six rubrics
so inserted by the original scribe. As a rule, in all later
cursive Greek MSS (I mean those of the seventh to the
fifteenth century) the ecclesiastical lections are indicated
throughout. Then either at the summit, or else at the foot
of the page, the formula with which the lection was to be
introduced is elaborately inserted, prefaced probably by a
rubricated statement (not always very easy to decipher) of
the occasion when the ensuing portion of Scripture was to
be read.

The ancients, to a far greater extent than ourselves, were
accustomed (in fact, they made it a rule) to prefix
unauthorized formulae to their public lections. These are
sometimes found to have established themselves so firmly
that at last they became as it were ineradicable, and later
copyists of the fourfold Gospel are observed to introduce
them unsuspiciously into the inspired text.

All that belongs to this subject deserves particular
attention, because it is this which explains not a few of the

perturbations (so to express oneself) which the text of the New Testament has experienced. We are made to understand how something that was originally intended only as a liturgical note became mistaken, through the inadvertence or the stupidity of copyists, for a critical suggestion. Thus, besides transpositions without number, there has arisen, at one time, the insertion of something unauthorized into the text of Scripture and at another time, the omission of certain inspired words, to the manifest detriment of the sacred deposit. For although the systematic rubrication of the Gospels for liturgical purposes is a comparatively recent invention (I question if it be older in Greek MSS than the tenth century), yet persons engaged in the public services of God's house have been prone, from the very earliest age, to insert memoranda of the kind referred to, into the margin of their copies.

In this way, in fact, it may be regarded as certain that in countless minute particulars the text of Scripture has been depraved. Let me not fail to add that by a judicious, and above all by an unprejudiced, use of the materials at our disposal, it may— even at this distance of time—in every such particular be successfully restored.

I now proceed to show, by an induction of instances, that even in the oldest copies in existence—I mean in Codices B and Aleph, A, C, and D—the lectionary system of the early Church has left abiding traces of its operation. When a few such undeniable cases have been adduced, all objections grounded on prima facie improbability will have been satisfactorily disposed of.

The activity as well as the existence of such a disturbing force and depraving influence, at least as far back as the beginning of the fourth century (but it is in fact more ancient by fully two hundred years), will have been established, I shall then only have to show, in conclusion, that the omission of the last twelve verses of St. Mark's Gospel is probably but one more instance of this force and influence, though confessedly by far the most extraordinary of any.

From Codex B, then, as well as from Codex A, the two grand verses which describe our Lord's "agony and bloody sweat" (St. Luke 22:43, 44) are missing. The same two verses are absent also from a few other important MSS, as well as from both the Egyptian versions; but I desire to fasten attention on the confessedly erring testimony in this place of Codex B.

"Confessedly erring," I say; for the genuineness of those two verses is no longer disputed. Now, in every known *Evangelistarium,* the two verses here omitted by Codex B follow (the Church so willed it) St. Matthew 26:39, and are read as a regular part of the lesson for the Thursday in Holy Week. Of course they are also omitted in the same *Evangelistaria* from the lesson for the Tuesday after Sexagesima, when St. Luke 22:39-23:1 used to be read.

If I do not insist that the absence of the famous *Pericope de Adultera* (St. John 7:53-8:11) from so many MSS is to be explained in precisely the same way, it is only because the genuineness of that portion of the Gospel is generally denied; and I propose, in this enumeration of instances, not to set foot on disputed ground.

I am convinced, nevertheless, that the first occasion of the omission of those memorable verses was the lectionary practice of the primitive Church, which, on Whitsunday, read from St. John 7:37 to 8:12, leaving out the twelve verses in question. Those verses, from the nature of their contents (as Augustine declares), easily came to be viewed with dislike or suspicion. The passage, however, is as old as the second century; for it is found in certain copies of the old Latin. Moreover, Jerome deliberately gave it a place in the Vulgate.

It has been proved, then, not only that ecclesiastical lections corresponding with those indicated in the *Synaxaria* were fully established in the immediately postapostolic age, but also that at that early period the lectionary system of primitive Christendom had already exercised a depraving influence of a peculiar kind on the text of Scripture.

Further yet (and this is the only point I am now concerned to establish), that our five oldest copies of the Gospels—B and Aleph as well as A, C, and D—exhibit not a few traces of the mischievous agency alluded to: errors, and especially omissions, which sometimes seriously affect the character of those codices as witnesses to the truth of Scripture.

I cannot dismiss the testimony of Eusebius until I have recorded my own entire conviction that this Father is no more an original authority here than Jerome or Hesychius or Victor. He is evidently adopting the language of some writer more ancient than himself. I observe that he introduces the problem with the remark that what follows is one of the questions "forever mooted by everybody." I suspect (with Matthaei) that Origen is the true author of all this confusion. He certainly relates of himself that among his voluminous exegetical writings was a treatise on St. Mark's Gospel.

To Origen's works, Eusebius (his apologist and admirer) is known to have habitually resorted. He is also known, like many others, to have derived not a few of his notions from that fervid and acute, but most erratic intellect. Origen's writings, in short, seem to have been the source of much if not most of the mistaken criticism of antiquity. (The reader is reminded of what has been offered above.) And this would not be the first occasion on which it would appear that when an ancient writer speaks of "the accurate copies," what he actually means is the text of Scripture which was employed or approved by Origen.

One more circumstance, and but one, remains to be adverted to in the way of evidence, and one more suggestion to be offered. The circumstance is familiar indeed to all, but its bearing on the present discussion has never been pointed out. I allude to the fact that anciently, in copies of the fourfold Gospel, the Gospel According to St. Mark frequently stood last.

This is memorably the case in respect of the Codex Bezae and more memorably yet in respect of the Gothic version of Ulphilas (A.D. 360). In both MSS the order of the Gospels is St. Matthew, St. John, St. Luke, and St. Mark. This is in fact the usual Western order. Accordingly it is thus that the Gospels stand in the Codices Vercelensis (a), Veronensis (b), Palatinus (e), and Brixianus (f) of the old Latin version.

But this order is not exclusively Western. It is found in Codex 309 and is also observed in Matthaei's Codices 13, 14 (which at last is our Evan. 256) at Moscow. And in the same order Eusebius and others of the ancients are occasionally observed to refer to the four Gospels, which induces a suspicion that they were not unfamiliar with it.

General Review of the Question, Summary of the Evidence, and Conclusion of the Whole Subject

This inquiry has at last reached its close. The problem was fully explained at the outset. All the known evidence has since been produced, every witness examined. Counsel has been heard on both sides. A just sentence will assuredly follow. But it may not be improper that I should in conclusion ask leave to direct attention to the single issue which has to be decided, and which has been strangely thrust into the background and practically kept out of sight by those who have preceded me in this investigation. The case stands simply as follows.

It being freely admitted that in the beginning of the fourth century there must have existed copies of the Gospels in which the last chapter of St. Mark extended no further than verse 8, the question arises, How is this phenomenon to be accounted for? . . . The problem is not only highly interesting and strictly legitimate, but it is even inevitable. In the immediately preceding chapter I have endeavored to solve it, and I believe in a wholly unsuspected way.

But the most recent editors of the text of the New Testament, declining to entertain so much as the possibility that certain copies of the second Gospel had experienced mutilation in very early times in respect of these twelve concluding verses, have chosen to occupy themselves rather with conjectures as to how it may have happened that St. Mark's Gospel was without a conclusion from the very first. Persuaded that no more probable account is to be given of the phenomenon that the Evangelist himself put forth a Gospel which (for some unexplained reason) terminated abruptly at the words *ephobounto gar* (chap. 16:8), they have unhappily seen fit to illustrate the liveliness of this conviction of theirs by presenting the world with his Gospel mutilated in this particular way. Practically, therefore, the question has been reduced to the following single issue: Whether of the two suppositions which follow is the more reasonable:

First, that the Gospel According to St. Mark, as it left the hands of its inspired Author, was in this imperfect or unfinished state, ending abruptly at (what we call now) the

8th verse of the last chapter—of which solemn circumstance, at the end of eighteen centuries, Codex B and Codex Aleph are the only surviving manuscript witnesses? . . . or,

Second, that certain copies of St. Mark's Gospel having suffered mutilation in respect of their twelve concluding verses in the postapostolic age, Codex B and Codex Aleph are the only examples of MSS so mutilated which are known to exist at the present day?

Editors who adopt the former hypothesis, are observed (a) to sever the verses in question from their context; (b) to introduce after verse 8 the subscription *"KATA MAPKON";* (c) to shut up verses 9-20 within brackets. Regarding them as "no integral part of the Gospel," "as an authentic anonymous addition to what Mark himself wrote down," a "remarkable fragment" placed as a completion of the Gospel in very early times," they consider themselves at liberty to go on to suggest that "the Evangelist may have been interrupted in his work"; at any rate, that "something may have occurred (as the death of St. Peter) to cause him to leave it unfinished." But "the most probable supposition," we are assured, "is that the last leaf of the original Gospel was torn away."

We listen with astonishment; contenting ourselves with modestly suggesting that surely it will be time to conjecture why St. Mark's Gospel was left by its Divinely inspired author in an unfinished state, when the fact has been established that it probably was so left. In the meantime, we request to be furnished with some evidence of that fact.

But not a particle of evidence is forthcoming. It is not even pretended that any such evidence exists. Instead, we are magisterially informed by "the first Biblical critic in Europe" (I desire to speak of him with gratitude and respect, but St. Mark's Gospel is a vast deal more precious to me than Dr. Tischendorf's reputation) that "a healthy piety reclaims against the endeavors of those who are for palming off as Mark's what the Evangelist is so plainly shown [where?] to have known nothing at all about."

In the meanwhile, it is assumed to be a more reasonable supposition (a) that St. Mark published an imperfect Gospel and that the twelve verses with which his Gospel concludes were the fabrication of a subsequent age than

(b) that some ancient scribe with design or by accident left out these twelve concluding verses, with the result that copies of the second Gospel so mutilated became multiplied and in the beginning of the fourth century existed in considerable numbers.

And yet it is notorious that very soon after the apostolic age, liberties precisely of this kind were freely taken with the text of the New Testament. Origen (A.D. 185-254) complains of the licentious tampering with the Scriptures which prevailed in his day. "Men add to them," he says, "or leave out, as seems good to themselves." Dionysius of Corinth, yet earlier (A.D. 168-176), remarks that it was no wonder his own writings were added to and taken from, seeing that men presumed to deprave the Word of God in the same manner. Irenaeus, his contemporary (living within seventy years of St. John's death), complains of a corrupted text.

We are able to go back yet half a century, and the depravations of Holy Writ become avowed and flagrant. A competent authority has declared it "no less true to fact than paradoxical in sound, that the worst corruptions to which the New Testament has been ever subjected originated within a hundred years after it was composed."

Above all, it is demonstrable that Codex B and Codex Aleph abound in unwarrantable omissions very like the present—omissions which do not provoke the same amount of attention only because they are of less moment. One such extraordinary depravation of the text, which also stands alone among MSS and to which its patrons are observed to appeal with triumphant complacency, has been already made the subject of distinct investigation. I am much mistaken if it has not been shown in my previous chapters that the omission of the words *en Ephesoi* from Ephesians 1:1 is just as unauthorized and quite as serious a blemish as the suppression of St. Mark 16:9-20.

Now in the face of facts like these and in the absence of any evidence whatever to prove that St. Mark's Gospel was imperfect from the first, I submit that a hypothesis so violent and improbable, as well as so wholly uncalled for, is simply undeserving of serious attention. It is plain from internal considerations that the improbability of the hypothesis is excessive, "the contents of these verses being such as to preclude the supposition that they were the work of a postapostolic period. The very difficulties which they present afford the strongest presumption of their genuineness." No fabricator of a supplement to St. Mark's Gospel would have ventured to introduce so many minute, seeming discrepancies; and certainly "his contemporaries would not have accepted and transmitted such an addition" if he had. It has also been shown at great length that the internal evidence for the genuineness of these verses is overwhelmingly strong.

Furthermore, even external evidence is not wanting. It has been acutely pointed out long since that the absence of a vast assemblage of various readings in this place is, in itself, a convincing argument that we have here to do with no spurious appendage of the Gospel. Were this a deservedly suspected passage, it must have shared the fate of all other deservedly (or undeservedly) suspected passages. It never could have come to pass that the various readings which these twelve verses exhibit would be considerably fewer than those which attach to the last twelve verses of any of the other three Gospels.

And then surely, if the original Gospel of St. Mark had been such an incomplete work as is feigned, the fact would have been notorious from the first and must needs have become the subject of general comment. It may be regarded as certain that so extraordinary a circumstance would have been largely remarked upon by the ancients, and that evidence of the fact would have survived in a hundred quarters.

It is, I repeat, simply incredible that tradition would have proved so utterly neglectful of her office as to remain quite silent on such a subject, if the facts had been such as are imagined. Either Papias or John the Presbyter, Justin Martyr or Hegesippus, or one of the *"Seniores apud Irenaeum"*—Clemens Alexandrinus or Tertullian or Hyppolytus—if not Origen, yet at least Eusebius, if not Eusebius, yet certainly Jerome—some early writer, I say, must certainly have recorded the tradition that St. Mark's Gospel, as it came from the hands of its inspired author, was an incomplete or unfinished work. The silence of the ancients, joined to the inherent improbability of the conjecture (that silence so profound, this improbability so gross!), is enough, I submit, in the entire absence of evidence on the other side, to establish the very contradictory of the alternative which recent critics are so strenuous in recommending to our acceptance.

But on the contrary, we have indirect yet convincing testimony that the oldest copies of all did contain the verses in question. And so far are any of the writers just enumerated from recording that these verses were absent from the early copies, that five out of those ten Fathers actually quote or else refer to the verses in question in a way which shows that in their day they were the recognized termination of St. Mark's Gospel.

We consider ourselves at liberty, therefore, to turn our attention to the rival alternative. Our astonishment is even excessive that it should have been seriously expected of us that we could accept without proof of any sort—without a particle of evidence, external, internal, or even traditional—the extravagant hypothesis that St. Mark put forth an unfinished Gospel. This is especially so since the obvious and easy alternative solicits us of supposing that at some period subsequent to the time of the Evangelist, certain copies of St. Mark's Gospel suffered that mutilation in respect of their last twelve verses of which we meet with no trace whatever, no record of any sort, until the beginning of the fourth century.

And the facts which now meet us on the very threshold are in a manner conclusive; for if Papias and Justin Martyr (A.D. 150) do not refer to them, yet certainly Irenaeus (A.D. 185) and Hippolytus (A.D. 190-227) distinctly quote six out of the two oldest Syriac Versions, as well as in the old Latin translation. Now the latest of these authorities is earlier by fully a hundred years than the earliest record that the verses in question were ever absent from ancient MSS. At the eighth Council of Carthage (as Cyprian relates), A.D. 256, Vincentius a Thiberi, one of the eighty-seven African bishops there assembled, quoted the 17th verse in the presence of the Council.

Nor is this all. Besides the Gothic and Egyptian Versions in the fourth century, and besides Ambrose, Cyril of Alexandria, Jerome, and Augustine in the fifth century, to say nothing of Codices A and C—the Lectionary of the Church universal, probably from the second century of our era, is found to bestow its solemn and emphatic sanction on every one of these twelve verses. They are met with in every MS of the Gospels in existence, uncial and cursive, except two; they are found in every version; and they are contained in every known Lectionary, where they are appointed to be read at Easter and on Ascension Day.

Early in the fourth century, however, we are encountered by a famous place in the writing of Eusebius (A.D. 300-340), who (as I have elsewhere explained) is the only Father who delivers any independent testimony on this subject at all. What he says has been strangely misrepresented. It is simply as follows.

One "Marinus" is introduced quoting this part of St. Mark's Gospel without suspicion, inquiring how its opening statement is to be reconciled with St. Matthew 28:1. Eusebius, in reply, points out that a man whose only object was to get rid of the difficulty might adopt the expedient of saying that this last section of St. Mark's Gospel "is not found in all the copies."

Declining, however, to act thus presumptuously in respect of anything claiming to be a part of evangelical Scripture, he enters at once without hesitation on an elaborate discussion to show how the two places may be reconciled. What there is in this to countenance the notion that in the opinion of Eusebius "the Gospel According to St. Mark originally terminated at the 8th verse of the last chapter," I profess myself unable to discover. I draw from his words the precisely opposite inference. It is not even clear to me that the verses in dispute were absent from the copy which Eusebius habitually employed. He certainly quotes one of those verses once and again.

On the other hand, the express statement of Victor of Antioch (A.D. 450?) that he knew of the mutilation but had ascertained by critical research the genuineness of this section of Scripture and had adopted the text of the authentic "Palestinian" copy, is more than enough to outweigh the faint presumption created (as some might think) by the words of Eusebius, that his own copy was without it.

And yet, as already stated, there is nothing whatever to show that Eusebius himself deliberately rejected the last twelve verses of St. Mark's Gospel. Still less does that Father anywhere say or even hint that in his judgment the original text of St. Mark was without them. If he may be judged by his words, he accepted them as genuine; for (what is at least certain) he argues upon their contents at great length, and apparently without misgiving.

It is high time however to point out that, after all, the question to be decided is not what Eusebius thought on this subject but what is historically probable. As a plain matter of fact, the sum of the patristic evidence against these verses is the hypothetical suggestion of Eusebius already quoted, which (after a fashion well understood by those who have given any attention to these studies) is observed to have rapidly propagated itself in the congenial soil of the fifth century.

And even if it could be shown that Eusebius deliberately rejected this portion of Scripture (which has never been done), yet, inasmuch as it may be regarded as certain that those famous codices in the library of his friend Pamphilus at Casarea, to which the ancients habitually referred, recognized it as genuine—the only sufferer from such a conflict of evidence would surely be Eusebius himself. It would not be St. Mark, I say, but Eusebius, who is observed to employ an incorrect text of Scripture on many other occasions and must (in such case) be held to have been unduly partial to copies of St. Mark in the mutilated condition of Codex B or Codex Aleph.

His words were translated by Jerome, adopted by Hesychius, referred to by Victor, and reproduced "with a difference" in more than one ancient scholion. But they are found to have died away into a very faint echo when Euthymius Zigabenus rehearsed them for the last time in his Commentary on the Gospels, A.D. 1116.

Exaggerated and misunderstood, behold them resuscitated after an interval of seven centuries by Griesbach, Tischendorf, Tregelles, and the rest: again destined to fall into a congenial, though very differently prepared soil, and again destined (I venture to predict) to die out and soon to be forgotten forever.

After all that has gone before, our two oldest codices (Codex B and Codex Aleph) which alone witness to the truth of Eusebius' testimony as to the state of certain copies of the Gospels in his own day, need not detain us long. They are thought to be as old as the fourth century; they are certainly without the concluding section of St. Mark's Gospel. But it may not be forgotten that both codices alike are disfigured throughout by errors, interpolations, and omissions without number; that their testimony is continually divergent; and that it often happens that where they both agree they are both demonstrably in error.

Moreover, it is a highly significant circumstance that the Vatican Codex (B), which is the more ancient of the two, exhibits a vacant column at the end of St. Mark's Gospel, the only vacant column in the whole codex. This shows that the copyist was aware of the existence of the twelve concluding verses of St. Mark's Gospel, even though he left them out; while the original scribe of the Codex Sinaiticus (Aleph) is declared by Tischendorf to have actually omitted the concluding verse of St. John's Gospel. It is due to this unenviable peculiarity that Aleph stands alone among MSS.

And thus we are brought back to the point from which we started. We are reminded that the one thing to be accounted for is the mutilated condition of certain copies of St. Mark's Gospel in the beginning of the fourth century, of which Codex B and Codex Aleph are the two solitary surviving specimens and Eusebius, are one historical witness.

We have to decide, I mean, between the evidence for this fact (namely, that within the first two centuries and a half of our era, the Gospel According to St. Mark suffered mutilation) and the reasonableness of the other opinion (namely, that St. Mark's original autograph extended no farther than chapter 16:8). All is reduced to this one issue. Unless any are prepared to prove that the twelve familiar verses (v. 9 to v. 20) with which St. Mark ends his Gospel cannot be his (I have proved on the contrary that he must needs be thought to have written them), I submit that it is simply irrational to persist in asseverating that the reason why those verses are not found in our two codices of the fourth century must be because they did not exist in the original autograph of the Evangelist.

What else is this but to set unsupported opinion, or rather unreasoning prejudice, before the historical evidence of a fact? The assumption is not only gratuitous, arbitrary, groundless; but it is discountenanced by the evidence of MSS, of versions, of Fathers (versions and Fathers much older than the fourth century), is rendered in the highest degree improbable by every internal and external consideration, and is condemned by the deliberate judgment of the universal Church. This Church, in its corporate capacity, for eighteen hundred years and in all places, has not only solemnly accepted the last twelve verses of St. Mark's Gospel as genuine, but has even singled them out for special honor.

Let it be asked in conclusion (for this prolonged discussion is now happily at an end), Are any inconveniences likely to result from a frank and loyal admission (in the absence of any evidence whatever to the contrary) that doubtless the last twelve verses of St. Mark's Gospel are just as worthy of acceptation as the rest? It might reasonably be supposed, from the strenuous earnestness with which the rejection of these verses is generally advocated, that some consideration must surely be assignable why the opinion of their genuineness ought on no account to be entertained. Do any such reasons exist? Are any inconveniences whatever likely to supervene?

No reasons whatever are assignable, I reply; neither are there any inconvenient consequences of any sort to be anticipated—except indeed to the critics. To them, it must be confessed, the result proves damaging enough.

It will only follow,

That Codex B and Codex Aleph must be henceforth allowed to be in one more serious particular untrustworthy and erring witnesses. They have been convicted, in fact, of bearing false witness in respect of St. Mark 16:9-20, where their evidence had been hitherto reckoned upon with the most undoubting confidence.

That the critical statements of recent editors, and indeed the remarks of critics generally, in respect of St. Mark 16:9-20, will have to undergo serious revision: in every important particular, will have to be unconditionally withdrawn.

That, in all future critical editions of the New Testament, these twelve verses will have to be restored to their rightful honors: nevermore appearing disfigured with brackets, encumbered with doubts, banished from their context, or molested with notes of suspicion. On the contrary. A few words of caution against the resuscitation of what has been proved to be a "vulgar error" will have henceforth to be introduced *in memoriam rei.*

Lastly, men must be no longer taught to look with distrust on this precious part of the deposit nor encouraged to dispute the Divine sayings which it contains on the plea that perhaps they may not be Divine, after all, or that probably the entire section is not genuine.

They must be assured, on the contrary, that these twelve verses are wholly undistinguishable in respect of genuineness from the rest of the Gospel of St. Mark; and it may not be amiss to remind them the creed called the "Athanasian" speaks no other language than that employed by the Divine Author of our religion and object of our faith. The Church warns her children against the peril incurred by as many as wilfully reject the truth, in no other language but that of the great Head of the Church. No person may presume to speak disparagingly of St. Mark 16:16 any more.

Whether, after the foregoing exposure of a very prevalent and highly popular, but at the same time most calamitous misapprehension, it will not become necessary for editors of the text of the New Testament to reconsider their conclusions in countless other places; whether they must not be required to review their method and to remodel their text throughout, now that they have been shown the insecurity of the foundation on which they have so confidently builded, and been forced to reverse their verdict in respect of a place of Scripture where at least they supposed themselves impregnable—I forbear at this time to inquire. Enough to have demonstrated, as I claim to have now done, that not a particle of doubt, that not an atom of suspicion, attaches to *The Last Twelve Verses of the Gospel According to St. Mark.*

I cannot so far forget the unhappy circumstances of the times as to close this note without the further suggestion (sure therein of the approval of our trans-Atlantic brethren) that, for a revision of the Authorized Version to enjoy the confidence of the nation and to procure for itself acceptance at the hands of the Church, it will be found necessary that the work should be confided to churchmen.

The Church may never abdicate her function of being "a witness and a keeper of Holy Writ." Neither can she, without flagrant inconsistency and scandalous consequence, ally herself in the work of revision with the sects. Least of all may she associate with herself in the sacred undertaking a Unitarian teacher—one who avowedly (see the letter of "One of the Revisionists, G.V.S.," in the *Times* of July 11, 1870) denies the eternal Godhead of her Lord.

That the individual alluded to has shown any peculiar aptitude for the work of a revisionist, or that he is a famous scholar, or that he can boast of acquaintance with any of the less familiar departments of sacred learning is not even pretended. (It would matter nothing if the reverse were the case.) What else, then, is this but to offer a deliberate insult to the Majesty of heaven in the Divine Person of Him who is alike the object of the everlasting Gospel and its author?

L'ENVOY

As one, escaped the bustling trafficking town,
Worn out and weary, climbs his favorite hill
And thinks it heaven to see the calm green fields
Mapped out in beautiful sunlight at his feet:
Or walks enraptured where the fitful south
Comes past the beans in blossom; and no sight
Or scent or sound but fills his soul with glee:
So I, rejoicing once again to stand
Where Siloa's brook flows softly, and the meads
Are all enamell'd o'er with deathless flowers,
And angel voices fill the dewy air.
Strife is so hateful to me! most of all
A strife of words about the things of God.
Better by far the peasant's uncouth speech
Meant for the heart's confession of its hope.
Sweeter by far in village school the words
But half remembered from the Book of Life,
Or scarce articulate lispings of the creed.

And yet, three times that miracle of spring
The grand old tree that darkens Exeter wall
Hath decked itself with blossoms as with stars,
Since I, like one that striveth unto death,
Find myself early and late and oft all day
Engaged in eager conflict for God's truth;
God's truth, to be maintained against man's lie.
And lo, my brook which widened out long since
Into a river, threatens now at length
To burst its channel and become a sea.

O sister, who ere yet my task is done
Art lying (my loved sister!) in thy shroud
With a calm, placid smile upon thy lips
As thou wert only "taking of rest in sleep,"
Soon to wake up to ministries of love,
Open those lips, kind sister, for my sake
In the mysterious place of thy sojourn.
(For thou must needs be with the bless'd, yea, where
The pure in heart draw wondrous nigh to God,)
And tell the Evangelist of thy brother's toil;
Adding (be sure!) "He found it his reward,

Yet supplicates thy blessing and thy prayers,
The blessing, saintly stranger, of thy prayers,
Sure at the least unceasingly of mine!"

One other landed on the eternal shore!
One other garnered into perfect peace!
One other hid from hearing and from sight! . . .
Oh, but the days go heavily, and the toil
Which used to seem so pleasant yields scant joy.
There come no tokens to us from the dead:
Save—it may be—that now and then we reap
Where not we sowed, and that may be from them,
Fruit of their prayers when we forgot to pray!
Meantime there comes no message, comes no word:
Day after day no message and no sign;
And the heart droops, and find that it was love
Not fame it longed for, lived for: only love.

JOHN W. BURGON

PERICOPE DE ADULTERA

John W. Burgon

PERICOPE DE ADULTERA*

A definitive, factual account of John 7:53-8:11 with positive
proof to show that it was in the original autographs of John's
Gospel

I have purposely reserved for the last the most difficult
problem of all: namely, those twelve famous verses of St.
John's Gospel (chap. 7:53-8:11) which contain the history
of "the woman taken in adultery"—the *Pericope de
Adultera,* as it is called.

It is altogether indispensable that the reader should
approach this portion of the Gospel with the greatest
amount of experience and the largest preparation. It would
be convenient, no doubt, if he could further divest himself
of prejudice; but that is perhaps impossible. Let him at
least endeavor to weigh in impartial scales the evidence
which will now be laid before him. He must do so of
necessity if he would judge rightly, for the matter to be
discussed is confessedly very peculiar and in some respects
even unique. Let me convince him at once of the truth of
what has been so far spoken.

It is a singular circumstance that at the end of eighteen
centuries two instances, and but two, should exist of a
considerable portion of Scripture left to the mercy (so to
speak) of textual criticism. Twelve consecutive verses in

*This material is taken from *The Causes of the Corruption of the Tradi-
tional Text of the Holy Gospels,* by John William Burgon, arranged, completed
and edited by Edward Miller (London: George Bell and Sons, 1896).

the second Gospel and as many consecutive verses in the
fourth are in this predicament.

It is singular, I say, that the Providence which has
watched so marvelously over the fortunes of the deposit,
the Divine wisdom which has made such ample provision
for its security all down the ages, should have so ordered
the matter that these two coextensive problems have
survived to our times to be tests of human sagacity—trials
of human faithfulness and skill. They present some striking
features of correspondence but far more of contrast, as will
presently appear.

And yet the most important circumstance of all cannot
be mentioned too soon namely, that both alike have
experienced the same calamitous treatment at the hands of
some critics. By common consent the most recent editors
deny that either set of verses can have formed part of the
Gospel as it proceeded from the hands of its inspired
author.

It has already been demonstrated in a separate treatise
how mistaken this opinion of theirs is in respect to the last
twelve verses of the Gospel According to St. Mark. I must
be content in this place to deal in a far less ceremonious
manner with the hostile verdict of many critics concerning
St. John 7:53-8:11.

That I shall be able to satisfy those persons who profess
themselves unconvinced by what was offered concerning
St. Mark's last twelve verses, I am not so simple as to
expect. But I trust that I shall have with me all candid
readers who are capable of weighing evidence impartially
and understanding the nature of logical proof when it is
fully drawn out before them, which indeed is the very
qualification I require of them.

And first, the case of the *Pericope de Adultera* requires
to be placed before the reader in its true bearings. For
those who have discussed it are observed to have ignored
certain preliminary considerations which, once clearly
apprehended, are all but decisive of the point at issue.
There is a fundamental obstacle, I mean, in the way of any
attempt to dislodge this portion of the sacred narrative
from the context in which it stands, which they seem to
have overlooked. I proceed to explain.

Sufficient prominence has never yet been given to the
fact that in the present discussion the burden of proof

rests entirely with those who challenge the genuineness of the *Pericope* under review. In other words, the question before us is not by any means, Shall these twelve verses be admitted into the sacred text or must they be refused admission? That point has been settled long, long ago. St. John's twelve verses are in possession. Let those eject them who can. They are known to have occupied their present position for fully seventeen hundred years. As far as is known, there never was a time when they were not where, and to all intents and purposes, they now are. Is it not evident that no merely ordinary method of proof, no merely common argument, will avail to dislodge twelve such verses as these?

Twelve such verses, I say. For it is the extent of the subject matter which makes the case so formidable. We have here to do with no dubious clause concerning which ancient testimony is divided, no seeming gloss which is suspected to have overstepped its proper limits and to have crept in as from the margin, no importation from another Gospel, no verse of Scripture which has lost its way, no weak amplification of the Evangelical meaning, no tasteless appendix which encumbers the narrative and almost condemns itself. Nothing of the sort.

If it were some inconsiderable portion of Scripture which it was proposed to get rid of by showing that it is disallowed by a vast amount of ancient evidence, the proceeding would be intelligible. But I take leave to point out that twelve consecutive verses of the Gospel cannot be so dealt with.

Squatters on the waste are liable at any moment to be served with a notice of ejectment, but the owner of a mansion surrounded by broad acres which his ancestors are known to have owned before the Heptarchy may on no account be dispossessed by any such summary process. This (to speak without a figure) is a connected and very striking portion of the sacred narrative: the description of a considerable incident, complete in itself, full of serious teaching, and of a kind which no one would have ever dared to invent. Those who would assail it successfully must come forward with weapons of a very different kind from those usually employed in textual warfare.

It will be presently shown that these twelve verses hold

their actual place by a more extraordinary right of tenure than any other twelve verses which can be named in the Gospel. It would, however, be premature to enter on the proof of that circumstance now. I prefer to invite the reader's attention next to the actual texture of the *Pericope de Adultera,* by which name (as already explained) the last verse of St. John 7 together with verses 1-11 of chapter 8 are familiarly designated.

Although external testimony supplies the sole proof of genuineness, it is nevertheless reasonable to inquire what the verses in question may have to say for themselves. Do they carry on their front the tokens of that baseness of origin which their impugners so confidently seek to fasten on them? Or do they, on the contrary, unmistakably bear the impress of truth?

The first thing which strikes me in them is that the actual narrative concerning the last nine of these verses: being preceded by two short paragraphs is of an entirely different character and complexion. Let these be first produced and studied:

> "and every man went to his own house: but Jesus went to the Mount of Olives." "And again, very early in the morning, he presented himself in the temple; and all the people came unto him: and he sat down and taught them."

Now as every one must see, the former of these two paragraphs is unmistakably not the beginning but the end of a narrative. It purports to be the conclusion of something which went before, not to introduce something which comes after. Without any sort of doubt, it is St. John's account of what occurred at the close of the debate between certain members of the Sanhedrin which terminates his history of the last day of the Feast of Tabernacles.

The verse in question marks the conclusion of the feast—implying, in short, that all is already finished. Remove it, and the antecedent narrative ends abruptly. Retain it, and all proceeds methodically, while an affecting contrast is established which is recognized to be strictly in the manner of Scripture. Each one had gone to his home, but the homeless One had repaired to the Mount of Olives.

In other words, the paragraph under discussion is found to be an integral part of the immediately antecedent narrative, proving to be a fragment of what is universally admitted to be genuine Scripture. By consequence, itself must needs be genuine also.

It is vain for anyone to remind us that these two verses are in the same predicament as those which follow: are as ill-supported by MS evidence as the other ten and must therefore share the same fate as the rest. The statement is incorrect, to begin with, as will presently be shown. But what is even more deserving of attention, since confessedly these twelve verses are either to stand or fall together, it must be candidly admitted that whatever begets a suspicion that certain of them at all events must needs be genuine, throws real doubt on the justice of the sentence of condemnation which has been passed in a lump on all the rest.

I proceed to call attention to another inconvenient circumstance which some critics in their eagerness have overlooked.

The reader will bear in mind that—contending, as I do, that the entire *Pericope* under discussion is genuine Scripture which has been forcibly wrenched away from its lawful context—I began by examining the upper extremity, with a view to ascertaining whether it bore any traces of being a fractured edge. The result is just what might have been anticipated. The first two of the verses which it is the fashion to brand with ignominy were found to carry on their front clear evidence that they are genuine Scripture. How then about the other extremity?

Note, that in the oracular Codexes B and Aleph immediate transition is made from the words "out of Galilee ariseth no prophet," in chapter 7:52, to the words "Again therefore Jesus spake unto them, saying," in chapter 8:12. And we are invited by all the adverse critics alike to believe that so the place stood in the inspired autograph of the Evangelist.

But the thing is incredible. Look back at what is contained between chapter 7:37 and 52, and note the following: two hostile parties crowded the temple courts (vv. 40-42); some were for laying violent hands on our Lord (v. 44); the Sanhedrin, being assembled in debate, were reproaching their servants for not having brought Him prisoner, and disputing one against another (vv. 45-52). How can the Evangelist have proceeded, "Again therefore Jesus spake unto them, saying, I am the light of the world"? What is it supposed then that St. John meant when he wrote such words?

But on the contrary, survey the context in any ordinary copy of the New Testament and his meaning is perfectly clear. The last great day of the Feast of Tabernacles is ended. It is the morrow and "very early in the morning." The Holy One has "again presented himself in the temple" where on the previous night He so narrowly escaped violence at the hands of His enemies, and He teaches the people.

While thus engaged—with the time, the place, His own occupation suggesting thoughts of peace and holiness and love—a rabble rout, headed by the scribes and Pharisees, enter on the foulest of errands; and we all remember with how little success. Such an interruption need not have occupied much time. The woman's accusers having departed, our Savior resumes His discourse which had been broken off.

"Again therefore" it is said in verse 12, with clear and frequent reference to what had preceded in verse 2: "Jesus spake unto them, saying, I am the light of the world." And did not that saying of His refer as well to the thick cloud of moral darkness which His words, a few moments before, had succeeded in dispelling, as to the orb of glory which already flooded the temple court with the effulgence of its rising—His own visible emblem and image in the heavens?

I protest that with the incident of "the woman taken in adultery," so introduced, so dismissed, all is lucid and coherent; without those connecting links, the story is scarcely intelligible. These twelve disputed verses, so far from "fatally interrupting the course of St. John's Gospel, if retained in the text," prove to be even necessary for the logical coherence of the entire context in which they stand.

But even that is not all. On close and careful inspection, the mysterious texture of the narrative, no less than its "edifying and eminently Christian" character, vindicates for the *Pericope de Adultera* a right to its place in the Gospel. Let me endeavor to explain what seems to be its spiritual significance; in other words, to interpret the transaction.

The scribes and Pharisees bring a woman to our Savior on a charge of adultery. The sin prevailed to such an extent among the Jews that the Divine enactments concerning one so accused had long since fallen into practical oblivion. On the present occasion our Lord is observed to revive His own ancient ordinance after a hitherto unheard of fashion. The trial by the bitter water, or water of conviction, was a species of ordeal intended for the vindication of innocence, the conviction of guilt. But according to traditional belief the test proved inefficacious, unless the husband was himself innocent of the crime whereof he accused his wife.

Let the provisions of the law, contained in Numbers 5:16-24, be now considered. The accused woman having been brought near and placed before the Lord, the priest took "holy water in an earthen vessel" and put "of the dust of the floor of the tabernacle into the water." Then, with the bitter water which causeth the curse" in his hand, he charged the woman by an oath. Next, he wrote the curses in a book and blotted them out with the bitter water, causing the woman to drink the "bitter water which causeth the curse." Whereupon if she were guilty, she fell under a terrible penalty, her body testifying visibly to her sin. If she was innocent, nothing followed.

And now, who sees not that the Holy One dealt with His hypocritical assailants as if they had been the accused parties? Verily they had been brought into the presence of incarnate Jehovah; and perhaps when He stooped down and wrote on the ground, it was a bitter sentence against the adulterer and adulteress which He wrote.

We have but to assume some connection between the curse which He thus traced "in the dust of the floor of the tabernacle" and the words which He uttered with His lips, and He may with truth be declared to have "taken of the dust and put in on the water" and "caused them to drink of the bitter water which causeth the curse." For when, by His Holy Spirit, our great High Priest in His human flesh addressed these adulterers, what did He but present them with living water "in an earthen vessel"?

Did He not further charge them with an oath of cursing, saying, "If ye have not gone aside to uncleanness, be ye free from this bitter water; but if ye be defiled. . . ." On being presented with this alternative, did they not, self-convicted, go out one by one? And what else was this but their own acquittal of the sinful woman, for whose condemnation they showed themselves so impatient? Surely it was "the water of conviction," as it is six times called, which they had been compelled to drink; whereupon, "convicted by their own conscience," as St. John relates, they had pronounced the other's acquittal.

Finally, note that by Himself declining to "condemn" the accused woman, our Lord also did in effect blot out those curses which He had already written against her in the dust, when He made the floor of the sanctuary His "book."

Whatever may be thought of the foregoing exposition (and I am not concerned to defend it in every detail), on turning to the opposite contention we are struck with the slender amount of actual proof with which the assailants of this passage seem to be furnished. Their evidence is mostly negative, a proceeding which is constantly observed to attend a bad cause; and they are prone to make up for the feebleness of their facts by the strength of their assertions.

But my experience, as one who has given a considerable amount of attention to such subjects, tells me that the narrative before us carries on its front the impress of Divine origin. I venture to think that it vindicates for itself a high, unearthly meaning. It seems to me that it cannot be the work of a fabricator. The more I study it, the more I am impressed with its Divinity. And in what goes before I have been trying to make the reader a partaker of my own conviction.

To come now to particulars, we may readily see from its very texture that it must needs have been woven on a heavenly loom. Only too obvious is the remark that the very subject matter of the chief transaction recorded in these twelve verses would be sufficient in and by itself to preclude the suspicion that these twelve verses are a spurious addition to the genuine Gospel.

And then we note how entirely in St. John's manner is the little explanatory clause in verse 6: "This they said, tempting him, that they might have to accuse him." We are struck besides by the prominence given in verses 6 and 8 to the act of writing, allusions to which are met with in every work of the last Evangelist.

It does not of course escape us how utterly beyond the reach of a Western interpolator would have been the insertion of the article so faithfully retained to this hour before *lithon* in verse 7. On completing our survey, as to the assertions that the *Pericope de Adultera* "has no right to a place in the text of the four Gospels," is "clearly a Western interpolation, though not Western of the earliest type" (whatever that may mean), and so forth. We can but suspect that the authors very imperfectly realize the difficulty of the problem with which they have to deal.

Dr. Hort finally assures us that "no accompanying marks would prevent" this portion of Scripture "from fatally interrupting the course of St. John's Gospel if retained in the text"; and when they relegate it accordingly to a blank page at the end of the Gospels within "double brackets" in order "to show its inferior authority," we can but read and wonder at the want of perception, not to speak of the coolness, which they display. *Quousque tandem?*

But it is time to turn from such considerations as the foregoing and inquire for the direct testimony, which is assumed by recent editors and critics to be fatal to these twelve verses. Tischendorf pronounces it "absolutely certain that this narrative was not written by St. John." One, vastly his superior in judgment (Dr. Scrivener), declares that "on all intelligent principles of mere criticism, the passage must needs be abandoned." Tregelles is "fully satisfied that this narrative is not a genuine part of St. John's Gospel." Alford shuts it up in brackets and, like Tregelles, puts it in his footnotes.

Westcott and Hort, harsher than any of their predecessors, will not, as we have seen, allow it to appear even at the foot of the page. To reproduce all that has been written in disparagement of this precious portion of God's written Word would be a joyless and unprofitable task. According to Green, "the genuineness of the passage cannot be maintained." Hammond is of opinion that "it would be more satisfactory to separate it from its present context and place it by itself as an appendix to the Gospel."

A yet more recent critic "sums up" that "the external evidence must be held fatal to the genuineness of the passage." The opinions of Bishops Wordsworth, Ellicott, and Lightfoot will be respectfully commented on by and by.

In the meantime, I venture to join issue with every one of these learned persons. I contend that on all intelligent principles of sound criticism the passage before us must be maintained to be genuine Scripture, and that without a particle of doubt. I cannot even admit that "it has been transmitted to us under circumstances widely different from those connected with any other passage of Scripture whatever." I contend that it has been transmitted in precisely the same way as all the rest of Scripture and therefore exhibits the same notes of genuineness as any other twelve verses of the same Gospel which can be named. Nevertheless, like countless other places it is found, for whatever reason, to have given offense in certain quarters; in consequence it has experienced very ill usage at the hands of the ancients and of the moderns also, but especially of the latter.

In other words, these twelve verses exhibit the required notes of genuineness less conspicuously than any other twelve consecutive verses in the same Gospel. But that is all. The only question to be decided is the following: On a review of the whole of the evidence, is it more reasonable to stigmatize these twelve verses as a spurious accretion to the Gospel or to admit that they must needs be accounted to be genuine? . . . I shall show that they are at this hour supported by a weight of testimony which is absolutely overwhelming. I read with satisfaction that my own convictions were shared by Mill, Matthaei, Alder, Scholz, and Vercollone. I have also the learned Ceriani on my side. I should have been just as confident had I stood alone—such is the imperative strength of the evidence.

To begin then. Tischendorf (who may be taken as a fair sample of the assailants of this passage) commences by stating roundly that the *Pericope* is omitted by Aleph A B C L T X △ and about seventy cursives. I will say that no sincere inquirer after truth could so state the evidence. It is in fact not a true statement. A and C are in this vicinity defective. It is therefore no longer possible to know with certainty what they either did or did not contain. But this is not merely all. I proceed to offer a few words concerning Codex A.

Woide, the learned and accurate editor of the Codex

Alexandrinus, remarked (in 1785), *"Historia adulterae videtur in hoc codice defuisse."* But this modest inference of his has been represented as an ascertained fact by subsequent critics. Tischendorf announces it as *"certissimum."*

Let me be allowed to investigate the problem for myself. Woide's calculation (which has passed unchallenged for nearly a hundred years, and on the strength of which it is nowadays assumed that Codex A must have exactly resembled Codices Aleph and B in omitting the *Pericope de Adultera*) was far too roughly made to be of any critical use.

Two leaves of Codex A have been here lost, namely, from the word *katabainon* in 6:50 to the word *legeis* in 8:52: a lacuna (as I find by counting the letters in a copy of the ordinary text) of as nearly as possible 8,805 letters, allowing for contractions and of course not reckoning St. John 7:53 to 8:11.

Now, in order to estimate fairly how many letters the two lost leaves actually contained, I have inquired for the sums of the letters on the leaves immediately preceding and succeeding the hiatus; and I find them to be respectively 4,337 and 4,303: a total of 8,640 letters. But this, it will be seen, is insufficient by 165 letters, or eight lines, for the assumed contents of these two missing leaves.

Are we then to suppose that one leaf exhibited somewhere a blank space equivalent to eight lines? Impossible, I answer. There existed, on the contrary, a considerable redundancy of matter in at least the second of those two lost leaves. This is proved by the circumstance that the first column on the next ensuing leaf exhibits the unique phenomenon of being encumbered, at its summit, by two very long lines (containing together fifty-eight letters), for which evidently no room could be found on the page which immediately preceded.

But why should there have been any redundancy of matter at all? Something extraordinary must have produced it. What if the *Pericope de Adultera,* without being actually inserted in full, was recognized by Codex A? What if the scribe had proceeded as far as the fourth word of St. John 8:3 and then had suddenly checked himself? We cannot tell what appearance St. John 7:53-8:11 presented in Codex A, simply because the entire leaf which should

have contained it is lost. Enough however has been said
already to prove that it is incorrect and unfair to throw
Aleph A B into one and the same category, with a *"certissimum,"* as Tischendorf does.

As for L and Δ, they exhibit a vacant space after St.
John 7:52, which testified to the consciousness of the
copyists that they were leaving out something. These are
therefore witnesses for—not witnesses against—the passage
under discussion. X being a commentary on the Gospel as
it was read in church, of course leaves the passage out. The
only uncial MSS therefore which simply leave out the
Pericope are the three following: Aleph B T. The degree of
attention to which such an amount of evidence is entitled
has already been proved to be wondrous small.

We cannot forget moreover that the two former of these
copies enjoy the unenviable distinction of standing alone
on a memorable occasion: they alone exhibit St. Mark's
Gospel mutilated in respect of its twelve concluding verses.

But I shall be reminded that about seventy MSS of later
date are without the *Pericope de Adultera;* that the first
Greek Father who quotes the *Pericope* is Euthymius in the
twelfth century; that Tertullian, Origen, Chrysostom,
Cyril, Nonnus, Cosmas, and Theophylact knew nothing of
it; and that it is not contained in the Syriac, Gothic, or
Egyptian Versions.

Concerning every one of these statements I remark over
again that no sincere lover of truth, supposing him to
understand the matter about which he is disputing, could
so exhibit the evidence for this particular problem. The
first reason is because so to state it is to misrepresent the
entire case. The next reason is because some of the articles
of indictment are only half true—in fact, are untrue. But
the chief reason is because in the foregoing enumeration
certain considerations are actually suppressed which, had
they been fairly stated, would have been found to reverse
the issue. Let me now be permitted to conduct this inquiry
in my own way.

The first thing to be done is to enable the reader clearly
to understand what the problem before him actually is.
The critics insist that twelve verses which, as a matter of
fact, are found dovetailed into a certain context of St.
John's Gospel, must be dislodged. But do the critics in
question prove that they must be? For unless they do,

there is no help for it but that the *Pericope de Adultera* must be left where it is.

I proceed to show, first, that it is impossible on any rational principle to dislodge these twelve verses from their actual context. Next, I shall point out that the facts adduced in evidence and relied on by the assailants of the passage do not by any means prove the point they are intended to prove, but admit of a sufficient and satisfactory explanation. Thirdly, it will be shown that the said explanation carries with it, and implies, a weight of testimony in support of the twelve verses in dispute that is absolutely overwhelming. Fourth, the positive evidence in favor of these twelve verses will be proved to outweigh largely the negative evidence, which is relied on by those who contend for their removal.

To some people I may seem to express myself with too much confidence. Let it then be said once for all that my confidence is inspired by the strength of the arguments which are now to be unfolded. When the Author of Holy Scripture supplies such proofs of His intentions, I cannot do otherwise than rest implicit confidence in them.

Now I begin by establishing as my first proposition that, these twelve verses occupied precisely the same position which they now occupy from the earliest period to which evidence concerning the Gospels reaches.

And this, because it is a mere matter of fact, is sufficiently established by reference to the ancient Latin version of St. John's Gospel. We are thus carried back to the second century of our era, beyond which testimony does not reach. The *Pericope* is observed to stand *in situ* in Codices b c e ff g h j. Jerome (A.D. 385), after a careful survey of older Greek copies, did not hesitate to retain it in the Vulgate. It is freely referred to and commented on by himself in Palestine; whereas Ambrose at Milan (374) quotes it at least nine times, as well as Augustine in North Africa (396) about twice as often. It is quoted besides by Pacian in the north of Spain (370), by Faustus the African (400), by Rufinus at Aquileia (400), by Chrysologus at Ravenna (433), and by Sedulius, a Scot (434).

The unknown authors of two famous treatises written at the same period largely quote this portion of the narrative. It is referred to by Victorius of Victorinus (457), by Vigilius of Tapsus (484) in North Africa, by Gelasius,

Bishop of Rome (492), by Cassiodorus in southern Italy, by Gregory the Great, and by other Fathers of the Western Church. (All references above referred to are found in *Causes of Corruption in the Traditional Text,* by Burgon and Miller.)

To this it is idle to object that the cited authors all wrote in Latin. For the purpose in hand their evidence is every bit as conclusive as if they had written in Greek— from which language no one doubts that they derived their knowledge, through a translation. But in fact we are not left to Latin authorities. (Out of thirty-eight copies of the Bohairic version the *Pericope de Adultera* is read in fifteen, but in three forms which will be printed in the Oxford edition. In the remaining twenty-three, it is left out.) How is it intelligible that this passage is thus found in nearly half the copies, except on the hypothesis that they formed an integral part of the Memphitic version? They might have been easily omitted, but how could they have been inserted?

Once more. The Ethiopic version (fifth century), the Palestinian Syriac (which is referred to the fifth century), the Georgian (probably fifth or sixth century), to say nothing of the Slavonic, Arabic, and Persian versions, which are of later date, all contain the portion of narrative in dispute. The Armenian version (fourth-fifth century) also originally contained it, though it survives at present in only a few copies. Add that it is found in Codex D, and it will be seen that in all parts of ancient Christendom this portion of Scripture was familiarly known.

But even this is not all. Jerome, who was familiar with Greek MSS (and who handled none of later date than B and Aleph), expressly related that the *Pericope de Adultera* "is found in many copies both Greek and Latin."

Whence is it—let me ask in passing—that so many critics fail to see that positive testimony like the foregoing far outweighs the adverse negative testimony of Aleph B T, yes, and of A C to boot, if they were producible on this point? How comes it to pass that the two codices, Aleph and B, have obtained such a mastery—rather exercise such a tyranny—over the imagination of many critics as quite to overpower their practical judgment?

We have at all events established our first proposition: namely, that from the earliest period to which testimony reaches, the incident of "the woman taken in adultery" occupied its present place in St. John's Gospel. The critics eagerly remind us that in four cursive copies (13, 69, 124, 346) the verses in question are found tacked onto the end of St. Luke 21. But have they then forgotten that "these four codices are derived from a common archetype" and therefore represent one and the same ancient and, may I add, corrupt copy?

The same critics are reminded that in the same four codices (commonly called the Ferrar Group) "the agony and bloody sweat" (St. Luke 22:43, 44) is found thrust into St. Matthew's Gospel between chapter 26:39 and 40. Such licentiousness on the part of a solitary exemplar of the Gospels no more affects the proper place of these or of those verses than the superfluous digits of a certain man of Gath avail to disturb the induction that to either hand of a human being appertain but five fingers, and to either foot but five toes!

It must be admitted then that as far back as testimony reaches, the passage under discussion stood where it now stands in St. John's Gospel. And this is my first position. But indeed, to be candid, hardly anyone has seriously called that fact in question. No, nor do any (except Dr. Hort) doubt that the passage is also of the remotest antiquity.

Adverse critics do but insist that however ancient, it must needs be of spurious origin or else it is an afterthought of the Evangelist. Concerning both of these imaginations we shall have a few words to offer by and by.

It clearly follows—indeed it may be said with truth that it only remains—to inquire what may have led to its so frequent exclusion from the sacred text? For really the difficulty has already resolved itself into that.

And on this head, it is idle to affect perplexity. In the earliest age of all—the age which was familiar with the universal decay of heathen virtue but which had not yet witnessed the power of the gospel to fashion society afresh and to build up domestic life on a new and more enduring basis; at a time when the greatest laxity of morals prevailed and the enemies of the gospel were known to be on the lookout for grounds of cavil against Christianity and its Author—what wonder if some were found to remove the *Pericope de Adultera* from their copies, lest it should be pleaded in extenuation of breaches of the seventh commandment?

The very subject matter, I say, of St. John 8:3-11 would sufficiently account for the occasional omission of those nine verses. Moral considerations abundantly explain what is found to have here and there happened. But in fact this is not a mere conjecture of my own. It is the reason assigned by Augustine for the erasure of these twelve verses from many copies of the Gospel.

Ambrose, a quarter of a century earlier, had clearly intimated that danger was popularly apprehended from this quarter; and Nicon, five centuries later, states plainly that the mischievous tendency of the narrative was the cause why it had been expunged from the Armenian version. Accordingly, just a few Greek copies are still to be found mutilated in respect of those nine verses only.

But in fact the indications are not a few that all the twelve verses under discussion did not by any means labor under the same degree of disrepute. The first three (as I showed at the outset) clearly belong to a different category from the last nine, a circumstance which has been too much overlooked.

In the meantime the Church, for an obvious reason, had made the choice of St. John 7:37-8:12—the greater part of which is clearly descriptive of what happened at the Feast of Tabernacles—for her Pentecostal lesson. And she judged it expedient, besides omitting as inappropriate to the occasion the incident of the woman taken in adultery, to ignore also the three preceding verses, thus making the severance begin, in fact, as far back as the end of chapter 7:52.

The reason for this is plain. In this way the allusion to a certain departure at night and return early next morning (St. John 7:53, 8:1) was avoided, which entirely marred the effect of the lection as the history of a day of great and special solemnity—"the great day of the feast." And thus it happens that the gospel for the day of Pentecost was made to proceed directly from "Search and look: for out of Galilee ariseth no prophet," in chapter 7:52, to "Then spake Jesus unto them, saying, I am the light of the world," in chapter 8:12, with which it ends.

In other words, an omission which owed its beginning to a moral scruple was eventually extended for a liturgical consideration and resulted in severing twelve verses of St. John's Gospel — chapter 7:53-8:11 — from their lawful context.

We may now proceed to the consideration of my second proposition, which is *That by the very construction of her Lectionary, the church in her corporate capacity and official character has solemnly recognized the narrative in question as an integral part of St. John's Gospel, and as standing in its traditional place, from an exceedingly remote time.*

Take into your hands at random the first MS copy of St. John's Gospel which presents itself and turn to the place in question. No, I will cite all the four Evangelia which I call mine, all the seventeen which belong to Lord Zouch, and all the thirty-nine which Baroness Burdett-Coutts imported from Epirus in 1870-1872. Now all these copies (and nearly each of them represents a different line of ancestry) are found to contain the verses in question. How did the verses ever get there?

But the most extraordinary circumstance of the case is behind. Some out of the Evangelia referred to are observed to have been prepared for ecclesiastical use. In other words, they are so rubricated throughout as to show where every separate lection had its "beginning" and where its "end."

Again I ask (and this time does not the riddle admit of only one solution?), When and how does the reader suppose that the narrative of "the woman taken in adultery" first found its way into the middle of the lesson for Pentecost? I pause for an answer. I shall of necessity be told that it never "found its way" into the lection at all; but having once crept into St. John's Gospel (however that may have been effected) and established itself there, it left those ancient men who devised the Church's Lectionary without choice. They could but direct its omission, and employ for that purpose the established liturgical formula in all similar cases.

But first, how is it that those who would reject the narrative are not struck by the essential foolishness of supposing that twelve fabricated verses, purporting to be an integral part of the fourth Gospel, can have so firmly established themselves in every part of Christendom from the second century downward, that they have long since become simply ineradicable?

Did the Church then, *pro hac vice,* abdicate her function of being "a witness and a keeper of Holy Writ"? Was she all of a sudden forsaken by the inspiring Spirit who, as she was promised, should "guide her into all truth"? And has she been all down the ages guided into the grievous error of imputing to the disciple whom Jesus loved a narrative of which he knew nothing?

For, as I remarked at the outset, this is not merely an assimilated expression, or an unauthorized nominative, or a weakly supported clause, or any such trifling thing. Although be it remarked in passing, I am not aware of a single such trifling excrescence which we are not able at once to detect and to remove. In other words, this is not at all a question, like the rest, about the genuine text of a passage. Our inquiry is of an essentially different kind, namely: Are these twelve consecutive verses Scripture at all, or not? Divine or human? They claim by their very structure and contents to be an integral part of the Gospel. And such a serious accession to the deposit, I insist, can neither have "crept into" the text nor have "crept out" of it. The thing is unexampled, is unapproached, is impossible.

Above all (the reader is entreated to give the subject his sustained attention), is it not perceived that the admission involved in the hypothesis before us is fatal to any rational pretense that the passage is of spurious origin? We have got back in thought at least to the third or fourth century of our era.

We are among the Fathers and Doctors of the Eastern Church in conference assembled, and they are determining what shall be the Gospel for the great Festival of Pentecost. "It shall begin," say they, "at the thirty-seventh verse of St. John 7, and conclude with the twelfth verse of St. John 8. But so much of it as relates to the breaking up of the Sanhedrin, to the withdrawal of our Lord to the Mount of Olives, and to His return next morning to the temple had better not be read. It disturbs the unity of the narrative.

"So also had the incident of the woman taken in adultery better not be read. It is inappropriate to the Pentecostal Festival." The authors of the great Oriental Liturgy therefore admit that they find the disputed verses in their copies, and thus they vouch for their genuineness.

For none will doubt that, had they regarded them as a spurious accretion to the inspired page, they would have said so plainly.

Nor can it be denied that if in their corporate capacity they had disallowed these twelve verses, such an authoritative condemnation would most certainly have resulted in the perpetual exclusion from the sacred text of the part of these verses which was actually adopted as a lection. What stronger testimony on the contrary can be imagined to the genuineness of any given portion of the everlasting Gospel than that it should have been canonized or recognized as part of inspired Scripture by the collective wisdom of the Church in the third or fourth century?

And no one may regard it as a suspicious circumstance that the present Pentecostal lection has been thus maimed and mutilated in respect to twelve of its verses. There is nothing at all extraordinary in the treatment which St. John 7:37-8:12 has here experienced. The phenomenon is even of perpetual recurrence in the Lectionary of the East.

Permit me to suppose that, between the Treasury and Whitehall, the remote descendant of some Saxon thane occupied a small tenement and garden which stood in the very middle of the ample highway. Suppose further, the property thereabouts being government property, that the road on either side of this estate had been measured a hundred times, and jealously watched, ever since Westminster became Westminster.

Well, an act of Parliament might no doubt compel the supposed proprietor of this singular estate to surrender his patrimony; but I submit that no government lawyer would ever think of setting up the plea that the owner of that peculiar strip of land was an impostor. The man might not have title deeds to produce, to be sure; but counsel for the defendant would plead that neither did he require any. "This man's title," counsel would say, "is—occupation for a thousand years. His evidences are—the allowance of the State throughout that long interval. Every procession to St. Stephen's, every procession to the Abbey has swept by defendant's property, on this side of it and on that, since the days of Edward the Confessor. And if my client refuses to quit the soil, I defy you—except by violence—to get rid of him."

It is in this way then that the testimony borne to these

verses by the Lectionary of the East proves to be of the most opportune and convincing character. The careful provision made for passing by the twelve verses in dispute, as well as the minute directions which fence those twelve verses off on this side and on that—directions issued we may be sure by the highest ecclesiastical authority, because recognized in every part of the ancient Church—establish them effectually in their rightful place. In addition, and what is at least of equal importance, these directions fully explain the adverse phenomena which are ostentatiously paraded by adverse critics and which, until the clue has been supplied, are calculated to mislead the judgment.

For now, for the first time, it becomes abundantly plain why Chrysostom and Cyril, in publicly commenting on St. John's Gospel, pass straight from chapter 7:52 to chapter 8:12. Of course they do. Why should they, how could they, comment on what was not publicly read before the congregation? The same thing is related (in a well-known scholion) to have been done by Apolinarius and Theodore of Mopsuestia. Origen's name, for aught I care, may be added to those who did the same thing, though the adverse critics have no right to claim him, seeing that his commentary on that part of St. John's Gospel is lost.

A triumphant refutation of the proposed inference from the silence of these many Fathers is furnished by the single fact that Theophylact must also be added to their number. Theophylact, I say, ignores the *Pericope de Adultera*— passes it by, I mean—exactly as do Chrysostom and Cyril. But will anyone pretend that Theophylact, writing in A.D. 1077, did not know of St. John 7:53-8:11? Why, in nineteen out of every twenty copies within his reach, the whole of those twelve verses must have been present.

The proposed inference from the silence of certain of the Fathers is therefore invalid. The argument *e silentio,* always an insecure argument, proves inapplicable in this particular case. When the antecedent facts have been once explained, all the subsequent phenomena become intelligible. But a more effectual and satisfactory reply to the difficulty occasioned by the general silence of the Fathers remains to be offered.

Underneath the appeal to patristic authority lies an opinion—not expressed indeed, yet consciously entertained by us all—which in fact gives the appeal all its weight and cogency, and which must now by all means be brought to the front.

The Fathers of the Church were not only her Doctors and teachers but also the living voices by which alone her mind could be proclaimed to the world, and by which her decrees used to be authoritatively promulgated. This fact makes their words, whenever they are delivered, so very important; their approval, if they approve, so weighty; their condemnation, if they condemn, so fatal.

But then, in the present instance, they neither approve nor condemn. They simply say nothing. They are silent; and in what precedes, I have explained the reason why. We wish it had been otherwise. We would give a great deal to persuade those ancient oracles to speak on the subject of these twelve verses, but they are all but inexorably silent.

No, I am overstating the case against myself. Two of the greatest Fathers (Augustine and Ambrose) actually do utter a few words; and they are to the effect that the verses are undoubtedly genuine: "Be it known to all men," they say, "that this passage is genuine; but the nature of its subject matter has at once procured its ejection from MSS and resulted in the silence of commentators." The most learned of the Fathers in addition practically endorses the passage; for Jerome not only leaves it standing in the Vulgate where he found it in the Old Latin version, but relates that it was supported by Greek as well as Latin authorities.

To proceed however with what I was about to say.

It is the authoritative sentence of the Church then on this difficult subject that we desiderate. We resorted to the Fathers for that, intending to regard any quotations of theirs, however brief, as their practical endorsement of all the twelve verses. We desired to infer from their general recognition of the passage that the Church in her collective capacity accepted it likewise.

As I have shown, the Fathers decline, almost to a man, to return any answer. But are we then without the Church's authoritative guidance on this subject? For this, I repeat, is the only thing we are in search of. It was only in order to get at this that we adopted the laborious expedient of watching for the casual utterances of any of the giants of old time. Are we, I say, left without the

Church's opinion?

Not so, I answer. The reverse is the truth. The great Eastern Church speaks out on this subject in a voice of thunder. In all her Patriarchates, as far back as the written records of her practice reach (and they reach back to the time of those very Fathers whose silence we felt to be embarrassing), the Eastern Church has selected nine out of these twelve verses to be the special lesson for October 8.

It would be impossible to adduce a more significant circumstance in evidence. Any pretense to fasten a charge of spuriousness on a portion of Scripture so singled out by the Church for honor is nothing else but monstrous. It would be in fact to raise quite a distinct issue, namely, to inquire what amount of respect is due to the Church's authority in determining the authenticity of Scripture? I appeal not to an opinion, but to a fact. That fact is, that though the Fathers of the Church for a very sufficient reason are nearly silent on the subject of these twelve verses, the Church herself has spoken with a voice of authority so loud that none can affect not to hear it. Indeed, it is so plain that it cannot possibly be misunderstood.

And let me not be told that I am hereby setting up the Lectionary as the true standard of appeal for the text of the New Testament; still less let me be suspected of charging on the collective body of the faithful whatever irregularities are discoverable in the codices which were employed for the public reading of Scripture. Such a suspicion could only be entertained by one who has failed to apprehend the precise point just now under consideration.

We are not examining the text of St. John 7:53-8:11. We are only discussing whether those twelve verses *en bloc* are to be regarded as an integral part of the fourth Gospel, or as a spurious accretion to it. And that is a point on which the Church in her corporate character must needs be competent to pronounce, and in respect of which her verdict must needs be decisive. She delivered her verdict in favor of these twelve verses, remember, at a time when her copies of the Gospels were of papyrus as well as "old uncials" on vellum. On the contrary, before "old uncials" on vellum were at least in any general use.

True, the transcribers of Lectionaries have proved them-

selves just as liable to error as the men who transcribed
Evangelia. But, then, it is incredible that those men forged
the Gospel for St. Pelagia's day; and it is impossible, if it
were a forgery, that the Church should have adopted it.
And it is the significance of the Church having adopted the
Pericope de Adultera as the lection for October 8, which
has never yet been sufficiently attended to, and which I
defy the critics to account for on any hypothesis but one:
namely, that the *Pericope* was recognized by the ancient
Eastern Church as an integral part of the Gospel.

Now when to this has been added what is implied in the
rubrical direction that a ceremonious respect should be
shown to the Festival of Pentecost by dropping the twelve
verses, I submit that I have fully established my second
position, namely, that by the very construction of her
Lectionary the Church in her corporate capacity and
official character has solemnly recognized the narrative in
question as an integral part of St. John's Gospel, and as
standing in its traditional place, from an exceedingly
remote time.

For (I entreat the candid reader's sustained attention),
the circumstances of the present problem altogether refuse
to accommodate themselves to any hypothesis of a
spurious original for these verses, as I proceed to show.

Repair in thought to any collection of MSS you
please—suppose to the British Museum. Request to be
shown their seventy-three copies of St. John's Gospel, and
turn to the close of his seventh chapter. At that particular
place you will find, in sixty-one of these copies, these
twelve verses; and in thirty-five of them you will discover,
after the words *Prophetēs ek tēs Galilaias ouk eg.* a rubrical
note to the effect that "on Whitsunday, these twelve verses
are to be dropped; and the reader is to go on at chapter
8:12."

What can be the meaning of this respectful treatment of
the *Pericope* in question? How can it ever have come to
pass that it has been thus ceremoniously handled down
through the ages? Surely on no possible view of the matter
but one can the phenomenon just now described be
accounted for. Else, will anyone gravely pretend to tell me
that at some indefinitely remote period (1) these verses
were fabricated; (2) were thrust into the place they at
present occupy in the sacred text; (3) were unsuspectingly

believed to be genuine by the Church; and in consequence they were at once passed over by her direction on Whitsunday as incongruous, and appointed by the Church to be read on October 8, as appropriate to the occasion?

But further. How is it proposed to explain why one of St. John's afterthoughts should have fared so badly at the Church's hands and another, so well? It is suggested that perhaps the subject matter may sufficiently account for all that has happened to the *Pericope de Adultera.* And so it may, no doubt. But then, once admit this, and the hypothesis under consideration becomes simply nugatory; it fails even to touch the difficulty it professes to remove.

For if men are capable of thinking scorn of these twelve verses when they found them in the "second and improved edition of St. John's Gospel," why may they not have been just as irreverent in respect of the same verses when they appeared in the first edition? How is it one whit more probable that every Greek Father for a thousand years should have systematically overlooked the twelve verses in dispute when they appeared in the second edition of St. John's Gospel, than that the same Fathers should have done the same thing when they appeared in the first?

But the hypothesis is gratuitous and nugatory; for it has been invented in order to account for the phenomenon that whereas twelve verses of St. John's Gospel are found in the large majority of the later copies, the same verses are observed to be absent from all but one of the five oldest codices.

But how (I wish to be informed) is that hypothesis supposed to square with these phenomena? It cannot be meant that the "second edition" of St. John did not come abroad until after Codices Aleph A B C T were written. For we know that the old Italic Version (a document of the second century) contains all the three portions of narrative which are claimed for the second edition. But if this is not meant, it is plain that some further hypothesis must be invented in order to explain why certain Greek manuscripts of the fourth and fifth centuries are without the verses in dispute. And this fresh hypothesis will render the one under consideration (as I said) nugatory and show that it was gratuitous.

What chiefly offends me however in this extraordinary suggestion is its irreverence. It assumes that the Gospel

According to St. John was composed like any ordinary modern book: capable therefore of being improved in the second edition, by recension, addition, omission, retraction, or what not. For we may not presume to limit the changes effected in a second edition. And yet the true Author of the Gospel is confessedly God the Holy Ghost, and I know of no reason for supposing that His works are imperfect when they proceed forth from His hands.

The cogency of what precedes has in fact weighed so powerfully with thoughtful and learned divines that they have felt themselves constrained, as their last resource, to cast about for some hypothesis which will at once account for the absence of these verses from so many copies of St. John's Gospel and yet retain them for their rightful owner and author, St. John.

Singular to relate, the assumption which has best approved itself to their judgment has been, that there must have existed two editions of St. John's Gospel—the earlier edition without, the later edition with, the incident under discussion. It is, I presume, in order to conciliate favor to this singular hypothesis that it has been further proposed to regard St. John 5:3, 4 and the whole of St. John 21 (besides St. John 7:53-8:11) as afterthoughts of the Evangelist.

But this is unreasonable, for nothing else but the absence of St. John 7:53-8:11 from so many copies of the Gospel has constrained the critics to regard those verses with suspicion.

Indeed, on the contrary, there is not known to exist a copy in the world which omits so much as a single verse of chapter 21. Why then are we to assume that the whole of that chapter was away from the original draft of the Gospel? Where is the evidence for so extravagant an assumption?

So, concerning St. John 5:3, 4, to which there really attaches no matter of doubt, as I have elsewhere shown, we find the following: thirty-two precious words in that place are indeed omitted by Aleph B C and twenty-seven by D. But by this time the reader knows what degree of importance is to be attached to such an amount of evidence. On the other hand, they are found in all other copies. They are vouched for by the Syriac and Latin Versions; in the Apostolic Constitutions, by Chrysostom,

Cyril, Didymus, and Ammonius; among the Greeks, by
Tertullian; among the Latins by Ambrose, Jerome, and
Augustine. Why a passage so attested is to be assumed an
afterthought of the Evangelist has never yet been
explained. Nor will it ever be.

Assuming, however, just for a moment the hypothesis
correct for argument's sake, namely, that in the second
edition of St. John's Gospel the history of the woman
taken in adultery appeared for the first time. Invite the
authors of that hypothesis to consider what follows. The
discovery that five out of six of the oldest uncials extant
(to reckon here the fragment T) are without the verses in
question, which yet are contained in ninety-nine out of
every hundred of the despised cursives: what other
inference can be drawn from such premises, but that the
cursives fortified by other evidence are by far the more
trustworthy witnesses of what St. John in his old age
actually entrusted to the Church's keeping?

THE LAST TWELVE VERSES
OF THE GOSPEL OF MARK

Samuel Zwemer

BIOGRAPHICAL SKETCH OF SAMUEL M. ZWEMER

Samuel Marinus Zwemer was the 13th of 15 children of French-Huguenot descent who fled to the Netherlands shortly after the revocation of the Edict of Nantes in 1685.

Known as the "Apostle to Islam", Samuel Zwemer studied medicine in preparation to his going to the mission field. While working in a New York clinic as an assistant to the druggist, he would usually attach a Scripture text to the bottle in which he had placed the medicine.

Once, in his haste, he forgot to look at the label on the bottle while he was about this "missionary task", but it wasn't long before a greatly upset patient had returned the bottle. On the bottle was the label "FOR EXTERNAL USE—POISON" and next to it the text "BE PREPARED TO MEET THY GOD"! His study of medicine, however, was to be the means to open many doors later on in his ministry in Arabia.

As he was a believer in the value of the printed page, Zwemer wrote many books. It is said that his books in English would fill a five-foot shelf. Many of his books have been translated into other languages such as: Arabic, Chinese, Dutch, French, German, Persian, Spanish, Swedish and Urdu. He was the founder-editor for 36 years of "The Moslem World" magazine. In many ways he resembled his predecessor in missionary labors,

Raymond Lull, who was the earliest well-known missionary to the Moslems.

While traveling in Shanghai, China in 1918 he received a cablegram from the President of Princeton Theological Seminary inviting him to become a member of the faculty. After ten years of teaching, he accepted a call to the Chair of History of Religion and Christian Missions.

Upon reaching the age of seventy years, he spoke to a group of students on the subject "Life Begins at Seventy". He mentioned the patriarchs and other great leaders who had accomplished their greatest work after three score years. Among his seven reasons why life began at seventy, Zwemer mentioned that: We should have a diploma from the school of experience by that time, at seventy we are near the river that has no bridge, and that at seventy years of age the Christian must redeem the time and live in more deadly earnest.

At the age of eighty, he revisted the mission fields where he had labored. He was a firm believer in the Bible as the very Word of God. Just ten days, April 2, 1952, before his eighty-fifth birthday, he passed away to be with His Lord.

THE LAST TWELVE VERSES
OF THE GOSPEL OF MARK

It has become the fashion to speak of the last twelve verses of St. Mark's Gospel as unauthentic. This critical conclusion, if it were valid, would leave the Gospel to end abruptly and rob us of the Great Commission as there recorded.

We are told that "the light thrown on the question by criticism, represented, e.g., by Tischendorf ... Zahn ... Westcott and Hort ... approaches certainty" *(Expositor's Greek Testament,* Vol. 1, p. 454). Dr. Alexander B. Bruce goes on to say in the work mentioned, that the external evidence strongly favors this conclusion. The section is wanting in two of the oldest manuscripts, Aleph and B. He quotes from Jerome and Eusebius that these verses are wanting in nearly all Greek copies, and then goes on to say: "The internal evidence of style confirms the impression made by the external; characteristic words of Mark are wanting; words not elsewhere found in the Gospel occur; the narrative is a meager, colorless summary, a composition based on the narratives of the other Gospels, and signs are ascribed to believers, some of which wear an apocryphal aspect."

Some, in spite of such considerations, still regard these verses as an integral part of Mark's work, but for many the question of present interest is: "What account is to be given of them viewed as an indubitable addendum by another hand?" There is no reference whatever to the elaborate vindication of the twelve verses of the Gospel

According to Mark by Dean John W. Burgon of Oriel College, Oxford. This devastating reply to all the critical objectors was published in 1871 and takes up in the greatest detail every argument advanced against the authenticity and genuineness of the passage.

F. C. Conybeare,[1] the same critic who assailed the genuineness of Matthew 28:19, also "discovered" the real author of the concluding verses of Mark. He is Aristion, the Presbyter, mentioned in an Armenian codex written about A.D. 986. And to satisfy pious folk who love the Gospels as they are, Dr. Bruce concludes his remarks on the Great Commission in Mark by saying: "Jesus may not have spoken as Matthew reports, but the words put into His mouth by the first evangelist are far more worthy of the Lord than those here ascribed to Him. Here also we find a great lapse from the high level of Matthew's version of the farewell words of Jesus: signs, physical charisms, and thaumaturgic powers, taking the place of the spiritual presence of the exalted Lord." (See also Meyer's *Commentary on Mark,* pp. 241-244.)

Those who use Dr. Moffatt's translation of the New Testament will find the same cavalier dismissal of these verses in Mark. He makes this Gospel end abruptly: "They said nothing to anyone for they were afraid of—"; then in a footnote he states that the reader has a choice of two appendices, second century attempts to complete what Mark left undone!

Now all this would be very interesting if it were true. But both external and internal evidence can be and has been brought together to show "that not a particle of doubt, that not an atom of suspicion, attaches to the last twelve verses of the Gospel According to Mark." These are the closing words of Dean Burgon's masterly monograph to which we will refer in some detail.

As regards the evidence of the manuscripts, we have much later arguments than that so carefully compiled in 1871 by Dean Burgon. Albert C. Clark, Corpus Professor of Latin at Oxford, in his book *The Primitive Text of the Gospels and Acts* (Oxford, 1914) summarizes his argument in a preface:

The method which I have here endeavored to apply to the criticism of the Gospels and Acts is one which took shape in the course of a previous investigation conducted upon the text of Cicero. . . . The test which I propose is arithmetical. It is based upon an empirical observation which I made while working upon the text of Cicero, namely, that short passages, the genuineness of which has been doubted on the ground of omission by a particular manuscript or family of manuscripts, frequently contain the same, or nearly the same, number of letters. I thus found myself in the presence of a unit. When I examined longer passages in the same way, I found multiples of this unit. The natural inference is that the unit corresponds to a line in an ancestor. . . . The chief result of my investigation has been to show the falsity of the principle *brevior lectio potior* (the shorter reading has stronger evidence). This was laid down by Griesbach as a canon of criticism. . . . Unless my method is based upon a delusion, this statement has no foundation in facts. I may also observe that it is not so easy to invent as it is to omit.

It will be understood that my work has been almost exclusively confined to the text of Cicero. It was only recently, after I had gained confidence in the use of my method, that, in a spirit of curiosity, I happened to apply it to the text of the Gospels. The results were so surprising that I gave up, for the present, my work upon Cicero, which can only interest a small circle, and devoted myself to this more important inquiry.

I must here state that when I began my investigation, I had not made any study of New Testament criticism. I had been brought up to look on the Revised Text as final, to smile at persons who maintained the authenticity of St. Mark 16:9-20, or St. John 7:53-8:11, etc., and to suppose that the "vagaries" of the "Western" text were due to wholesale interpolation. The object which I had in view was merely to study the mutual relations of the oldest Greek uncials, notably, the *Vaticanus* (B), the *Sinaiticus* (Aleph), and the *Alexandrinus* (A). I was, however, soon dislodged from this arrogant attitude, and irresistibly driven to very different conclusions.

These I can only briefly indicate here, and must refer the reader to my subsequent discussion for the evidence. Nowhere is the falsity of the maxim *brevior lectio potior* more evident than in the New Testament. The process has been one of contraction, not of expansion. The primitive text is the longest, not the shortest. It is to be found not in B, Aleph, or in the majority of Greek manuscripts, but in the "Western" family, i.e., in the ancient versions and the Codex Bezae (D). If my analysis is sound, we are brought back to an archetype of the four Gospels in book form, which cannot be later than the middle of the second century. This archetype appears to have contained the passages which have been most seriously suspected by recent critics, e.g., the end of St. Mark and St. John 7:53-8:11.[2]

The reader will pardon the length of these quotations because they are important and they also bring us to the heart of the problem, namely, the fact that Codex B of the Vatican Library and Codex Aleph brought from Mount Sinai in 1859 do not contain the last twelve verses of Mark. This was the principal reason why Tischendorf, Tregelles, and Alford denied their genuineness. So when Westcott and Hort issued their revised text of the New Testament, they assured us that "the original text terminated abruptly, from whatever cause ... the rest was added at another time and probably by another hand." Meyer insists that verses 9-19 are an apocryphal fragment and reproduces the so-called external and internal evidence.

We desire to give a summary of the arguments of Dean John Burgon (in a book that proved as interesting to us as a detective story), and then to return briefly to the contention of Clark with which we began and later evidence.

The question is of comparatively recent date, for Griesbach was the first (1796-1806) to insist that the concluding verses were spurious.

The early Fathers, to the number of nineteen, including Papias, Justin Martyr, and Irenaeus, witness to these verses in their writings. Some of these are quotations—it is true, fragmentary—but others are complete. Ambrose cites verses 16-18 three times. Jerome gives all the twelve verses their place in the Vulgate. And these nineteen witnesses represent every part of the ancient Church, from Antioch to Rome and Carthage. Seven of them are of more ancient date than the oldest codex we posses.[3]

The early versions are also examined and found to yield unfaltering testimony to the genuineness of these verses. The Peshitta, the Vetus Itala, the Vulgate, the Gothic, and the Egyptian Versions all contain the passage in question. The main contradictory testimony is the Armenian Version, whose codices are of more recent date. "Thus we are in possession of the testimony of at least six independent witnesses of a date considerably anterior to the earliest extant codex of the Gospels. Their testimony to the genuineness of these verses is unfaltering."

In Chapter 5, Burgon deals with the alleged hostile witness of certain early Fathers, such as Eusebius, Gregory of Nyssa, and Jerome. These are examined one by one in the most painstaking manner and we cannot escape the conclusion of Burgon:

> Six Fathers of the Church have been examined who are commonly represented as bearing hostile testimony to the last twelve verses of St. Mark's Gospel; and they have been easily reduced to one. Three of them (Hesychius, Jerome, Victor) prove to be echoes, not voices. The remaining two (Gregory of Nyssa and Severus) are neither voices nor echoes, but merely *names,* Gregory of Nyssa having really no more to do with this discussion than Philip of Macedon, and "Severus" and "Hesychius" representing one and the same individual. Only by a critic seeking to mislead his reader will any one of these five Fathers be in future cited as witnessing against the genuineness of St. Mark 16:9-20.

> Eusebius is the solitary witness who survives the ordeal of exact inquiry. But Eusebius (as we have seen), instead of proclaiming his distrust of this portion of the Gospel, enters on an elaborate proof that its contents are not inconsistent with what is found in the Gospels of St. Matthew and St. John.

His testimony is reducible to two innocuous and wholly unconnected propositions: the first—that there existed in his day a vast number of copies in which the last chapter of St. Mark's Gospel ended abruptly at verse 8 (the correlative of which, of course, would be that there also existed a vast number which were furnished with the present ending); the second—that by putting a comma after the word *"Anastas,"* St. Mark 16:9 is capable of being reconciled with St. Matthew 28:1 (pp. 65-66).

In Chapter 6 of Burgon the manuscript testimony is shown to be overwhelmingly in favor of these verses. They are contained in every important manuscript in the world except two. However, neither Codex B nor Codex Aleph is infallible but both contain omissions and interpolations. Eighteen uncials and six hundred cursive manuscripts of this Gospel contain the verses in question. The superstitious reverence for Codex B is unwarranted. (A. C. Clark comes to the same conclusion on entirely other grounds, based not on the text as such but on stichometry and the proof of omissions by copyists.) Burgon gives several examples (pp. 73-75) and then he concludes:

To say that in the Vatican Codex (B), which is unquestionably the oldest we possess, St. Mark's Gospel ends abruptly at the eighth verse of the sixteenth chapter, and that the customary subscription *(KATA MAPKON)* follows, is true; but it is far from being the whole truth. It requires to be stated in addition that the scribe, whose plan is found to have been to begin every fresh book of the Bible at the top of the next ensuing column to that which contained the concluding words of the preceding book, has at the close of St. Mark's Gospel deviated from his else invariable practice. He has left in this place one column entirely vacant. It is the only vacant column in the whole manuscript—a blank space abundantly sufficient to contain the twelve verses which he nevertheless withheld. Why did he leave that column vacant? What can have induced the scribe on this solitary occasion to depart from his established rule? The phenomenon (I believe I was the first to call distinct attention to it) is in the highest degree significant, and admits of only one interpretation. The older manuscript from which Codex B was copied must have infallibly contained the twelve verses in dispute. The copyist was instructed to leave them out—and he obeyed; but he prudently left a blank space *in memoriam rei.* Never was blank more intelligible! Never was silence more eloquent! By this simple expedient, strange to relate, the Vatican Codex is made to refute itself even while it seems to be bearing testimony against the concluding verses of St. Mark's Gospel, by withholding them; for it forbids the inference which, under ordinary circumstances, must have been drawn from that omission. It does more. By leaving room for the verses it omits, it brings into prominent notice at the end of fifteen centuries and a half, a more ancient witness than itself (pp. 86, 87).[4]

After replying to certain other objections based on ancient scholia and notes in manuscripts, Burgon turns to the internal evidence for and against the genuineness of the passage.

The style and phraseology of Mark are absent from the closing paragraphs, so we are told by the critics; and therefore they are not genuine. Here Burgon is at his best and the scores of pages devoted to a devastating reply simply fascinate the reader who has any knowledge whatever of Greek. He turns the tables completely against the critics; and with fairness, but marvelous skill, he demonstrates that all of the instances given of style and language prove exactly the opposite of what is intended.

One critic puts it: "There is a difference so great between the use of language in this passage and its use in the undisputed portion of Mark's Gospel as to furnish strong reasons for believing the passage not genuine." Scrivener, on the other hand, refused to pay any attention whatever "to the argument against these twelve verses, arising from their alleged difference in style" (Intro., pp. 431-432). Professor John A. Broadus of the Southern Baptist Seminary also wrote an able and convincing paper refuting the assertion that the style and language of the passage in question argued for its spuriousness *(The Baptist*

Quarterly, July, 1869).

The argument of Burgon is as follows: There are twenty-seven alleged words and phrases listed by the critics as peculiar. These twenty-seven alleged difficulties of style and vocabulary he discusses one by one. They include a variation of the word for Sabbath (v. 9) and the mention of Mary Magdalene (as one from whom demons were cast, v. 9), whereas in the same chapter she is twice referred to without this statement! The preposition used after "casting out demons" is peculiar. The word for "go" used three times (vv. 10, 12, 15) is not used elsewhere by Mark.

But the fact is that compounds of this Greek word are used by him frequently—twenty-four times, that is, oftener than in all the other Gospels! The expression "those with him" is peculiar (v. 10). However, Mark here refers not to the eleven but to the larger company of believers as in Acts 20:18 and Luke 24:9. This expression therefore is rather a proof of an eyewitness and of Mark's peculiarity of giving detail.

And so the record goes on of the other words that occur only once, or are peculiar in this section. But why this suspicion of the possibility that an author can use new words or use them in a new sense occasionally?

Finally, after fifty pages of painstaking patience with this hypercriticism of style, and after showing that in fact there are twenty-seven notes of genuineness, based on style and vocabulary, in this very short passage, Burgon concludes:

> Something more is certain than that the charges which have been so industriously brought against this portion of the Gospel are without foundation. It has been proved that, scattered up and down these twelve verses, there actually exist twenty-seven other words and phrases which attest with more or less certainty that those verses are nothing else but the work of the Evangelist (p. 173).

Professor Broadus tells how it occurred to him to use the preceding twelve verses (Mark 15:44-16:8) for critical study, and he discovered here seventeen peculiar words not found elsewhere in Mark! A *reductio ad absurdum (Baptist Quarterly,* July, 1869). So the whole argument from style is rendered weak and the test breaks down hopelessly under severe analysis.

This section of Dean Burgon's book has special value because he was known as one of the greatest Greek scholars of his day. Born in Smyrna in 1813, the son of a merchant living in Turkey, educated in London University and Oxford, he became Professor of Divinity and, later, Dean of Chichester, where he died in 1888. He was known in Oxford as "the champion of lost causes" and was the author of scores of books and articles on New Testament textual criticism. (See Schaff-Herzog and the British Museum Catalogue.)

Conybeare himself expressed his indebtedness to Dean Burgon's monograph and states his opinion that "perhaps no one so well sums up the evidence for and against" these concluding verses of Mark *(The Expositor,* 4, viii [1913], p. 241). As far as I can learn, no adequate reply to Dean Burgon has ever been written. Nor is Dean Burgon the only, although he is the chief, scholar to contend for the genuineness of Mark 16:9-20.[5]

Dr. Henry Barclay Swete, in his commentary on the Gospel of Mark (1905), devotes ten pages to a discussion of the twofold ending of the text. He admits the alleged difficulties of the problem but states: "The documentary testimony for the longer ending is, as we have seen, overwhelming. Nevertheless, there are points at which the chain of evidence is not merely weak but broken." However, he quotes Dr. Salmon as saying: "We must ascribe their authorship to one who lived in the very first age of the Church. And why not to St. Mark?"

And in another paragraph, Dr. Swete asserts: "Thus on the whole it seems safe to conclude that at Rome and at Lyons in the second half of the second century the Gospel ended as it does now. If the last twelve verses did not form part of the autograph, there is nothing to show when they were attached to the Gospel. But they must have been very generally accepted as the work of St. Mark soon after the middle of the second century, if not indeed at an earlier time. It is significant that a writer of such wide knowledge as Irenaeus entertained no doubt as to their genuineness."

The strongest argument for and against the twelve verses always goes back to the two manuscripts B and Aleph, but in spite of their age there are reasons for doubting their authority in this instance. A. C. Clark does so on the ground of their frequent omissions. He bases his argument on stichometry. Reviewing his book, the London *Times* said: "No critic henceforth can refuse to take account of this book; and the worship of the short text had the rudest shock it has met with for years. If with Westcott and Hort and their followers we regard the shorter, neutral text as primitive, we certainly lose much in the Gospels that has had the most tender and sacred associations for countless generations of believers."

Professor Clark draws attention to the fact that a large number of the words and phrases absent from Westcott and Hort's text consist of ten to twelve Greek letters, or multiples of that number; and when in the manuscript they were set out in narrow columns, the reason for these omissions is obvious. The same word or syllable occurred just before or just after, and so the scribe skipped one or more lines—but always the same multiple. Clark has no theological prejudice and is no partisan for any particular manuscript, but as a brilliant Latin scholar of the text of Cicero applies the same principles to the New Testament text and his verdict is for the genuineness of Mark 16:9-20.

Finally, Dean Burgon assails the authority of B and Aleph on the ground of their skeptical character. (See Appendix V, p. 288, *The Traditional Text of the Holy Gospels.*) There seems to be an alliance between them and the school of Origen. In the Gospel text they omit those words and phrases that emphasize the Divinity of our Lord. He gives twenty-three examples. I Timothy 3:16 is a typical instance: *Hos* for *Theos;* the omission of passages that relate to everlasting punishment, e.g., Mark 9:44, 46 and 3:29; omission of the strengthening angel in Gethsemane (Luke 22:43, 44) and the first word from the cross (Luke 23:34); mutilation of the Lord's Prayer (Luke 11:2-4); and so forth. The reader of this section is convinced that the Western text, so-called, is undoubtedly more conservative than that of B and Aleph.

In Appendix V, Burgon lists 76 passages in which manuscripts of the B-Aleph type betray their skeptical character. D follows them in only 35 instances, and in this respect is "more conservative" than B-Aleph.

In addition to all this, Edward Miller, editor of the posthumous work of Burgon, points out that even as in B, so in Aleph we have proof in the very manuscript itself that the writer was conscious of having made an important omission at the end of Mark. "The scribe manages to conclude Mark not with a blank column such as in B tells its own story, but with a column such as in this manuscript is usual at the end of a book, exhibiting the closing words, followed by an arabesque pattern executed with the pen and the subscription.

"But by the very pains he has taken to conform this final column to the ordinary usage of the manuscript his purpose of omission is betrayed even more conclusively, though less obviously, than by the blank column of B" (Appendix VII, *The Traditional Text of the Holy Gospels,* pp. 299-300). This observation is due to Dr. Salmon who comments on it in his *Historical Introduction* (5th ed., p. 147). The discussion is most interesting especially in connection with the findings of A. C. Clark to which we have already referred.

But the most astonishing statement of all refers to the alleged twofold witness of B and Aleph. It occurs on page 233 of *The Traditional Text of the Holy Gospels:*

> The last twelve verses of St. Mark's Gospel, according to Drs. Westcott and Hort, are spurious. But what is their ground of confidence? for we claim to be as competent to judge of testimony as they. It proved to be "the unique criterion supplied by the concord of the independent attestations of Aleph and B."

> "Independent attestations"! But when two copies of the Gospel are confessedly derived from one and the same original, how can their "attestations" be called "independent"? This is however greatly to understate the case. The nonindependence of B and Aleph in respect of St. Mark 16:9-20 is absolutely unique; for, strange to relate, it so happens that the very leaf on which the end of St. Mark's Gospel and the beginning of St. Luke's is written (St. Mark 16:2-Luke 1:56), is one of the six leaves of Codex Aleph which are held to have been written by the scribe of Codex B. "The inference," remarks Scrivener, "is simple and direct, that at least in these leaves Codices B and Aleph make

but one witness, not two" (Miller and Burgon, *Tradi-tional Text,* p. 233).

In Scrivener's Introduction (Vol. 2, pp. 337-338) he refers to the work of Burgon and argues for the genuine ness of the passage. Here are his words:

> Dean Burgon's brilliant monograph, *The Last Twelve Verses of the Gospel According to St. Mark Vindi-cated Against Recent Objectors and Established* (Oxford and London, 1871), has thrown a stream of light upon the controversy, nor does the joyous tone of his book misbecome one who is conscious of hav-ing triumphantly maintained a cause which is very precious to him. We may fairly say that his conclu-sions have in no essential point been shaken by the elaborate and very able counterplea of Dr. Hort (Notes, pp. 28-51).

While completing this paper my attention was called to a far more recent study on the genuineness of the last twelve verses of Mark's Gospel. It is by the Roman Catholic theologian Gerhard Hartmann, S.J., and appeared in a series of New Testament studies published at Munster in 1936 (Band XVII, pp. 175-275). This meticulous and scholarly examination of the whole question occurs as an appendix to his study on the sources of Mark (Aufbau) and is entitled *Untersuchungen zur Echtheit des Markus-Schlusses,* u.s.w.

He pays special attention to the Greek words of the passage in question and shows how all arguments based on them fall to the ground when we examine the structure as well as the vocabulary of Mark. This evangelist everywhere emphasizes faith, and in these twelve verses he refers to faith and unbelief in Christ's resurrection eight times. One by one Hartmann examines the words that supposedly are an argument against genuineness and turns every alleged difficulty into a witness for the authenticity of these closing verses! The objections raised to the signs and miracles as postapostolic he meets by referring to Mark 11:23 and Mark 6:13, where the faith of the disciples works even greater signs. And then he devotes thirty pages to the history of the Greek text and the witness of the manuscripts, confirming and supplementing the conclusion of Dean Burgon written sixty years earlier.

A word should be added regarding the evidence for the genuineness of the Great Commission as found in one of the Freer Manuscripts. This is designated as Codex W and was discovered at Akhmim in Upper Egypt and purchased from Ali Arabi by Charles Lang Freer of Washington, D.C., in 1907. It goes back to the fourth or fifth century and has a different ending to Mark than that of the accepted text. (See Moffatt's N.T. translation for the full text.)

In this case the passage given within brackets by Moffatt is new but the verses that precede and follow are exactly like the text which we call the Authorized Version, namely, verses 12-14 and 15-20. These are the very verses that include the Great Commission unaltered and the command to baptize. A facsimile photostat of the two sides of this leaf of Codex W is given by Caspar Rene Gregory in his book, and after critical study he designates the additional paragraph as "not genuine words of Jesus."[6] So here is further evidence of the Received Text and its genuineness from the Freer Manuscript as interpreted by a great authority on New Testament textual criticism.

After all this we are content to turn to the text of the Authorized English Version, to scores of translations made by the Bible Societies into hundreds of languages and rejoice to find in them no break and no mutilation of the Mark text. And as for "the signs" that will follow these who believe, all of which the critics reject as thaumaturgic and fantastic (v. 17), we are content with the miracles of missions, since the day when Paul shook off the viper at Melita to. the experiences of David Livingstone in Africa, the exorcising of demons in China,[7] and the providential deliverances among the headhunters of Borneo in our own day. The Lord is still working with His apostles and "confirming the word with signs following. Amen."

NOTES

[1] His *History of New Testament Criticism* (London 1910) was issued for the Rationalist Press Association.

[2] Clark, who contended that many short omissions in the manuscripts of the B-Aleph class were the result of "stichometric" omission, was also convinced by other considerations that these longer passages in Mark and John had a place in the original text. From an entirely different angle a Russian New Testament student, Dr. Ivan Panin, comes to a similar conclusion. He spent many years in a meticulous study of the "numerical value and structure of the Old and New Testament text." In his *Numeric Greek New Testament* (Oxford University Press, 514 pp.), he lists twenty-three numeric features beneath the surface of Mark 16:9-20 that tend to prove it genuine. His method is by many considered bizarre

if not absurd. (See the *Sunday School Times*, September 3, 1941, and reply, December 26, 1942.) There is a copy of his rare and privately printed book on *The Last Twelve Verses of Mark: Their Genuineness Established* (Ontario, Aldershort, 1930) in the New York Public Library.

3 In *The Traditional Text of the Holy Gospels* (London, 1896), a posthumous work of Dean Burgon, edited by Edward Miller, we have the following list of the witnesses for the traditional ending of Mark's Gospel (p. 109): Papias (Eus. H. E. 3:39); Justin Martyr (Tryph. 53; Apol. i. 45); Irenaeus (c. Haer. III. x. 6; iv. 56); Tertullian (De Resurr. Carn. xxxvii; Adv. Praxeam xxx); Clementines (Epit. 141); Hippolytus (c. Haer. Noet, ad fin); Vincentius (Second Council of Carthage—Routh, Rell. Sacr. iii. p. 124); Acta Pilati (xiv. 2); Apost. Can. and Const. (can. i; v. 7; 19; vi. 15; 30; viii. 1); Eusebius (Mai, Script. Vett. Nov. Collect. i. p. 1); Cyril Jerus. (Cat. xiv. 27); Syriac Table of Canons; Macarius Magnes (iii. 16; 24); Aphraates (Dem. i—bis); Didymus (Trin. ii. 12); Syriac Acts of the Apostles; Epiphanius (Adv. Haer. l. xliv. 6); Gregory Nyss. (In Christ. Resurr. ii); Apocryphal Acts of the Gospel—Wright (4; 17; 24); Ambrose (Hexameron vi. 38; De Interpell. ii. 5; Apol. proph. David II. iv. 26; Luc. vii. 81; De Poenit. I. viii. 35; De Spir. S. II. xiii. 151); The only contradictory evidence in the Fathers is that of Eusebius (Mai, Script. Vett. Nov. Collect. i. p. 1).

4 Dean Burgon's conclusions were corroborated in two posthumous volumes, *The Traditional Text of the Holy Gospels* and *The Causes of the Corruption of the Traditional Text of the Holy Gospels*, by Edward Miller. London, 1895-1896.

5 In *Hastings' Dictionary of the Bible* we find: "The longer conclusion is supported by the vast majority of uncials, including A, C, D, E, F, G, H, K, M, S, U, V, X, etc., by the cursives in a body, most of them giving the paragraph xvi. 9-20 without note, twenty or more of them stating that it was found in the best manuscripts, though it was wanting in some; by all the Lectionaries for Easter and Ascension Day, by the Old Latin and Vulgate Versions, the Curetonian, Peshitta, Harcleian, and Jerusalem Syriac . . . and by many of the Fathers, including Justin (possibly), Irenaeus, Eusebius, Epiphanius, Didymus, Nestorius, Ambrose, Augustine, and most Latin writers after these, as well as by the Apostolic Constitutions, the Gesta Pilati, the Syrian Aphrates, etc."

6 Von Caspar Rene Gregory, *Das Freer-Logion*, Leipzig, 1908, pp. 18, 31, 61, 62, 64. See also Albert Clark, *The Primitive Text*, pp. 76, 77.

7 See John L. Nevius, *Demon Possession* (Grand Rapids: Kregel Publications, Reprint edition, 1968).

THE PRESERVATION OF THE SCRIPTURES

Donald L. Brake

Condensed by
David Otis Fuller

THE PRESERVATION OF THE SCRIPTURES*

Introduction

Perhaps the greatest theological battles of the present day are fought in the area of Bibliology. This is especially true of the doctrines of inspiration and inerrancy. The orthodox doctrine of inspiration declares that the Holy Scriptures are God-breathed and were originated by Him. Inerrancy maintains that in the original manuscripts the Scriptures were without error.

Certain liberals have taken inspiration to be an inspiring of the Scriptures toward man. Henry writes, "Barth emphasizes the 'inspiring' of Scripture, that is, its present use by the Holy Spirit towards hearers and readers."[1] Most liberals deny completely the inerrancy of Scripture. Rauschenbusch writes concerning inerrancy, "There are many degrees of clarity and power in this living inspiration, and heavy admixtures of human error."[2]

The Christian Church, however, has from the beginning predominately accepted the original autographs of the books of the Old and New Testaments as inspired by God through the Holy Spirit. Irenaeus in the second century wrote, "The Scriptures are indeed perfect; they were certainly spoken by the Word of God and His Spirit."[3] Augustine continued the same thought when he wrote, "For I do not account Cyprian's writings as canonical, but weigh them by the canonical Scriptures; and that in them which agreeth with canonical I allow to his praise; but that

*This article comprises in edited form, the thesis presented to the faculty of the Department of Systematic Theology at Dallas Theological Seminary in partial fulfillment of the requirements for the Degree, Master of Theology under the title, *The Doctrine of the Preservation of the Scriptures* by Donald L. Brake, May 1970. Used by permission of Dallas Theological Seminary.

that agreeth not, by his favor I refuse."[4] Calvin wrote:

> But since we are not favored with daily oracles from
> heaven, and since it is only in the Scriptures that the
> Lord hath been pleased to preserve his truth in
> perpetual remembrance; it obtains the same complete
> credit and authority with believers, when they are
> satisfied of its Divine origin, as if they heard the very
> words pronounced by God himself.[5]

For the early Christians to say that the Scriptures were
inspired was also to affirm that they were inerrant.

Since it is maintained by orthodox Christians that the
Scriptures were written in their original form without
error, it is reasonable to maintain that they have been
Divinely preserved. Burgon writes:

> There exists no reason for supposing that the Divine
> Agent, who in the first instance thus gave to mankind
> the Scriptures of truth, straightway abdicated His
> office; took no further care of His work; abandoned
> those precious writings to their fate.[6]

If the text of the Scriptures was not preserved, what was
the need for having an inerrant original? Martin, quoting
an unidentified source, writes:

> What is the use of the inspiration of the Bible, if no
> form of the Bible that we now have is inspired? Why
> should God have worked a stupendous miracle in
> order to preserve the writers of the Biblical books
> from error and make the autographs of their books
> completely true, if He intended then to leave the
> books thus produced to the mere chance of trans-
> mission from generation to generation by very human
> and often careless copyists? [7]

Many modern textual critics fall into a mistake similar
to Beegle when they rely so heavily upon Codex Sinaiticus
(Aleph) and Codex Vaticanus (B), both fourth century
uncial manuscripts. In effect they are saying that the autographs were given inerrantly, but we have no form of an
inerrant text today since all manuscripts contain errors.

Therefore, some may say, preservation guarantees only a text of "essential" purity.

The text which underlies many of the modern English versions (e.g., RSV and ASV) is based primarily on two nineteenth century manuscripts—Sinaiticus and Vaticanus. Prior to the discovery of these two manuscripts the standard text was the *Textus Receptus.*

The manuscripts underlying the *Textus Receptus* were late, but they represented the overwhelming majority of all extant manuscripts. But the majority of textual critics today believe that God preserved His text through the manuscripts discovered in the nineteenth century. They are saying, in effect, that God kept hidden from the Church the true text of the Word of God from some time around the ninth century until the discoveries of Codex Sinaiticus and Vaticanus in the nineteenth century. Burgon writes of how unlikely it is for God to have hidden His true text for such a long period:

> I am utterly disinclined to believe—so grossly improbable does it seem—that at the end of eighteen hundred years 995 copies out of every thousand, suppose, will prove untrustworthy; and that the one, two, three, four, or five which remain, whose contents were till yesterday as good as unknown, will be found to have retained the secret of what the Holy Spirit originally inspired.[8]

The issue ultimately is: Has God preserved throughout history a continuous, uninterrupted text for the Church or has He merely preserved for one thousand years a corrupted text and then revealed His true text when a German critic at the convent of St. Catherine picked out of a wastebasket one single manuscript?

It is my purpose to demonstrate that God has Divinely preserved His text in a continuous, uninterrupted tradition; that modern textual critics have overestimated the value of Aleph and B; and that within our manuscript tradition we possess every word which God recorded in the original manuscripts. This pure text may be secured by patient and diligent counting of manuscripts to determine which reading is the majority reading. When there are some variants which are equally distributed among the manuscripts, no judgment can be made until further collation of manuscripts has been made.

The scriptural basis for the doctrine will be discussed in some detail, giving attention to direct references, implied evidences, and its basis in the character of God.

The history of the preservation of the text will constitute an important part of the paper, showing that God has Divinely preserved His Word. Textual criticism will be discussed from the viewpoint of its importance in preserving the text.

In the chapter which discusses the preserved text of the New Testament, evidence will be given historically, textually, and logically for the traditional text as being the text through which God has chosen to preserve His Word.

The study will not include the development of the canon in history, although it is also important to the doctrine, since any study of that would be only a survey and there are many fine treatments of the subject in standard texts.

The doctrine of verbal, plenary inspiration will be assumed and no attempt will be made to vindicate its claim. Inspiration is absolutely essential to preservation. Without inspiration the defense of preservation would be impossible.

I

THE BASIS FOR THE DOCTRINE OF PRESERVATION

The Biblical Basis

The doctrine of the preservation of the Scriptures was not stated in any creed of the Church until the Westminster Confession of Faith in 1646. As the first creed to set forth the doctrine in written form, it was precise and exacting: "being immediately inspired by God, and, by His singular care and providence kept pure in all ages."[9] In 1675 the Helvetic Consensus Formula was even more precise:

God saw to it that His word, which is with power unto salvation to everyone who believes, was entrusted to writing not only through Moses, the prophets and apostles but also He has stood guard and watched over it with a fatherly concern to the present time that it not be destroyed by the cunning of Satan or by any other human deceit.[10]

The doctrine of preservation is not, however, a doctrine which was begun or introduced in the Westminster Confession. It has its basis in the Scriptures themselves.

The doctrine of preservation does not guarantee the preservation of the autographs, for they perished within a few years after their writing. Neither does it guarantee the accuracy of the copies, because errant men copied them. It does guarantee, however, that the complete contents of the Scriptures have been preserved, not in any one manuscript, but somewhere within the manuscript tradition. Martin writes, "No one of them in itself is absolutely accurate, for God has not guaranteed the infallibility of any copyist, but the infallible words are there somewhere within those manuscripts."[11]

Direct Biblical Evidence

There are a number of references in both the Old and New Testament which give evidence for the doctrine of preservation. These are not all direct proof-texts, but evidence that imply God's Word is enduring, everlasting, or settled in heaven; therefore, it is reasonable that He has preserved His Word in written form.

Psalm 119:89 declares, "For ever, O Lord, thy word is settled in heaven." The verse declares that the Word of God is as stable as heaven itself. Delitzsch writes:

Eternal and imperishable in the constant verifying of itself is the vigorous and consolatory Word of God, to which the poet will ever cling. It has heaven as its standing-place, and therefore it also has the qualities of heaven and before all others, heaven-like stability.[12]

The meaning of the verse becomes obvious. The Word which is settled in heaven was placed there by a deliberate and purposeful act of God Himself.

Isaiah 40:8 adds the thought of endurance to the concept of the stability of the Word: "The grass withereth, the flower fadeth: but the word of our God shall stand for ever."

Isaiah 40 begins the third major section of the prophecy of Isaiah. It has as its general theme the idea of comfort while awaiting deliverance. In verses 1 through 11 Isaiah tells the nation of the endurance of God's Word, which becomes a source of comfort. The theme of verses 1 through 11 is the proclamation of the perishable nature of all flesh and the imperishable nature of the Word of God, which is proclaimed by a voice (presumably not of the prophet Isaiah). "What comes out of man's mouth is uncertain and temporary, but what God speaks is as eternal as His very character."

Matthew 5:17-18—The Lord Jesus speaks of the preservation of the Scriptures when He attributes greater stability to the law than to the heavens and the earth: "For verily I say unto you, Till heaven and earth pass, one jot or one tittle shall in no wise pass from the law, till all be fulfilled." Lightner writes:

> If the Savior was teaching anything at all by these words "jot" and "tittle" and the fact of their durability, He was teaching that the most minute portions and trifles of the Old Testament as originally written, the very markings which gave meanings to words of Scripture, would not fail of fulfillment because they came from God and were thus absolutely inerrant.[13]

"The law" does not refer only to the laws and ordinances of Judaism but rather to the sacred Scriptures which recorded them. As Lightner puts it, "Christ's reference to the law does not only mean the ordinances of Judaism because nothing of those ordinances would be known apart from the record in Scripture."[14]

Someone may object to making the term "law" in verse 18 refer to the Scriptures, even though it is the obvious meaning of the law and the prophets of verse 17. The terms "jot" and "tittle" are designations for written material. To whatever the law refers, it is *written,* or else the use of "jot" and "tittle" would not be meaningful. The law, whatever its reference, is a written portion of God's Word; and it will endure at least until the end of the heavens and earth.

Chafer points out that there is little difference between the written Word and the spoken Word:

It may be pointed out that there is practically no difference in the essential reality of the spoken Word and the written Word, for one is no more than a form in which the other appears. Both are like the breath of His mouth. [15]

There seems to be in Matthew 5:17-18 a limitation set by the phrase "till heaven and earth pass." Is the Word, then, preserved only until the end of the heavens and earth? This may be answered easily if one sees the phrase as an idiom used by the Jews when making reference to unlimited duration.

John 10:35—The context of the passage reveals that Christ had just claimed to be God; and the Jews, having recognized His claim, were about to put Him to death. In His own defense Christ appeals to the Scriptures. The phrase "and the Scripture cannot be broken" is a reply to His own question which was brought up in the quoting of Psalm 82. The reason He could appeal to Scripture in defending Himself was that the Scriptures could not be broken. Lightner speaks succinctly on this phrase:

The word "cannot" expresses a Divine and moral impossibility. The point is, Scripture cannot be annulled, dissolved, abrogated, or rendered void because it declares the will and purpose of God. Of equal importance in Christ's statement is the word "broken." By this expression He emphasizes not only the Divine authority but also the unity and solidarity of Scripture. [16]

Young writes:

The concept of breaking a law is one that is clearly comprehended. If a man breaks a law, he is guilty and so liable to punishment. When he breaks a law, the lawbreaker treats the law as nonexistent, and in effect annuls it. The Scriptures, however, possess an authority so great that they cannot be broken. What they say will stand and cannot be annulled or set aside.[17]

The important element which is added by John 10:35 and was not as specific in the previous verses, is that it mentions the Scriptures by name. It maintains that the Scriptures cannot cease to exist, that they will stand. It is as direct and forceful as possible in maintaining the preservation of the Scriptures.

I Peter 1:23-25—The basic truth of this passage is that the doctrine of the Word of God stimulates love for our brethren. One of the reasons for loving the brethren is that we have been born again. Just as the Word of God lives and abides forever, so also should be the character and nature of our love for the brethren.

The major problem of the passage is to determine the meaning of "the Word of God." Some have taken the phrase to refer to the Christian dispensation. Shedd writes: "It denotes the gospel dispensation, like the 'word of truth' in James 1:18. Christians are born again of incorruptible seed, namely of the Holy Spirit, under the Christian dispensation."[18] Others have limited the phrase to refer to the Christian gospel, equating it with verse 25 where the Word is said to be the gospel: "But the word of the Lord endureth for ever. And this is the word which by the Gospel is preached unto you."

Indirect Biblical Evidence

The importance of preservation of Christ's arguments. Christ depended completely on the authority of the Scriptures in many of His encounters with the scribes and Pharisees. In most of these encounters He depended entirely on a word or phrase from the Old Testament to support His argument. In each case it was absolutely necessary that He be quoting or reading the exact account which had been recorded in the original manuscripts. He had complete confidence that He was quoting the correct text. It was necessary, then, for the Old Testament Scriptures to have been preserved down through the centuries and in some cases even to the very words themselves.

In John 10:34-36 Christ is quoting from Psalm 82:6. The context of the passage reveals that Christ's enemies had come to Him at Solomon's porch to demand an answer as to whether or not He was the Messiah. Jesus replied by declaring to them the miracles which He had done by Divine power. If they were in sympathy with Him they would have believed from the miracles.

Then Christ comes out with a clear claim that He and the Father are one. The Jews, recognizing His claim of Deity, took up stones to kill Him. Christ defends Himself from the Psalms. He says in effect that since the Hebrew Scriptures teach that judges who represented God in that office could be called "gods," then why could not He be the Son of God who was the complete revelation of God in His Divine mission? Christ's argument rested on the fact that the Old Testament Scriptures had been preserved.

The importance of preservation to prophecy. There are many prophecies that were fulfilled in Christ's time which depended entirely on the preservation of one word in Scripture. Such a prophecy is found in Micah 5:2 which states, "But thou, Bethlehem Ephratah, though thou be little among the thousands of Judah, yet out of thee shall he come forth unto me that is to be ruler in Israel; whose goings forth have been from of old, from everlasting." The prophecy is quoted in Matthew 2:5 as having been the place of the birth of Christ. The quotation of the prophecy of Micah depends entirely on the one word "Bethlehem," which is recorded in both passages.

The importance of preservation in Paul's arguments. Paul depended on the singular form of one word for his argument in Galatians 3:16. In this passage Paul is defending the doctrine of justification by faith. He is attempting to show that the principle has never changed. The Jews were insisting that the law of Moses was binding on the descendants of Abraham because it came subsequent to the promise of Abraham. They wanted to place obedience to the law beside justification by faith in Christ. Paul emphasizes the singular form of a word to show that the true fulfillment of the Abrahamic promise was in Christ. Verse 16 reads: "Now to Abraham and his seed were the promises made. He said not, and to seeds, as of many; but as of one, and to thy seed, which is Christ." He is insisting that the promise was not to all the descendants of

Abraham but to one, who is Christ; and 3:29 adds that all who are of Christ are the heirs of the promise.

The entire argument of Paul rests on the preservation of the singular form of the term "seed." Paul was confident that the word "seed" was the inspired form which had been recorded in the original and preserved in the text to which he was referring.

Most of the evidence advanced to this point has been primarily concerned with the preservation of the Scriptures and has referred mostly to the Old Testament. One step is yet to be bridged in the argument. Can the New Testament be considerd Scripture?

Peter, who of all men should have had the most against Paul because of Paul's rebuke for his eating with the Gentiles and attempting to hide it from the Jews, placed Paul's writings on an equal basis with the Old Testament Scriptures: "As also in all his [Paul's] epistles . . . as they do also the other Scripture unto their own destruction" (II Peter 3:16).

In II Timothy 5:18 Paul writes: "For the scripture saith, Thou shalt not muzzle the ox that treadeth out the corn. And, the labourer is worthy of his reward." Paul has quoted from Deuteronomy 25:4 ("Thou shalt not muzzle the ox when he treadeth out the corn") and from Luke 10:7 ("for the labourer is worthy of his hire"), calling both Scripture. Paul is claiming in a natural way that to him the Book of Luke is just as sacred as the Old Testament. It follows, therefore, that the rest of the Gospels are also Scripture.

The Basis in the Character of God

Some conservative scholars today do not believe that the doctrine of preservation has any connection with the moral character of God. John Skilton, faculty member at Westminster Theological Seminary, writes:

> We will grant that God's care and providence, singular though they have been, have not preserved for us any of the original manuscripts either of the Old Testament or of the New Testament. We will furthermore grant that God did not keep from error those who copied the Scriptures during the long period in which the sacred text was transmitted in copies written by

hand. But we must maintain that the God who gave the Scriptures, who works all things after the counsel of his will has exercised a remarkable care over his Word, has preserved it in all ages in a state of essential purity, and has enabled it to accomplish the purpose for which he gave it.[19]

It is true that God has not permitted any of the original manuscripts to be preserved. The reason for it has been left to speculation. Perhaps God did not wish for them to become objects of veneration. Whatever the reason, God in His providence permitted all the original manuscripts to perish.

The second point of Skilton's words seems at first glance to be quite logical and correct. The idea of "essential purity" appears to have a great deal to commend it. The question which comes to mind at once on close scrutiny is just how "essential purity" agrees with the doctrine of the Word as the instrument of salvation.[20] Does this mean, then, that a person can only be absolutely sure about such large areas of truth? As was stated earlier, why then is there a need for a doctrine of inerrancy? How can it be known about any given passage that it is indeed the very words of God?

Although separate doctrines, the doctrine of preservation is very closely connected to the doctrine of inerrancy. Preservation is necessary in order to maintain an adequate view of inerrancy. Without preservation, the doctrine of inerrancy is only an academic question and has little bearing on the formation of doctrine and exegesis. Hills writes:

The providential preservation of the Scriptures is also a necessary consequence of their Divine inspiration. The God who inspired the Scriptures and gave them to His people to be their authoritative guide and consolation cannot allow this perfect and final revelation of His will to perish. Because God has inspired the Scriptures, He has also preserved them by His providence.[21]

It would never be said that what is in the Greek texts would lead one into error in doctrine or practice; yet if preservation is not held, one could be misled in certain passages due to the difference of words.

Many theologians such as Young[22] and Skilton[23] believe that the doctrine of preservation guarantees only that no point of doctrine has been affected. The fact is that there are passages where variant readings do make a difference in doctrine. In I Corinthians 15:51, where Paul elaborates on the doctrine of the resurrection, the variants do make a difference to that doctrine. B and the vast majority of Greek manuscripts read: "We shall not all sleep, but we shall all be changed." But Aleph, A, C, F, and G read: "We shall all sleep, but we shall not all be changed." D adds to the variants: "We shall all rise, but we shall not all be changed." The Chester Beatty Papyrus reads: "We shall not all sleep, nor shall we all be changed.[24] It is true that for the most part the differences are small and do not affect doctrine, but there are differences that do affect doctrine.

It is incredible to think that a God who Divinely inspired the writings of the autographs so that every word was without error, would then leave His Holy Word in the hands of sinful and imperfect men who could miscopy and perhaps lose some of His words so that in a matter of a few years the Scriptures would no longer be inerrant. The statement that the words of God "will endure forever" shows that it is quite safe to maintain that the Scriptures recording these words will be preserved from their inception to their consummation—forever.

The Biblical basis for any doctrine is vital; however, particular proof-texts cannot always be given. It has been demonstrated that the Scriptures teach that the Word of God has an eternal endurance. Although in many cases the Biblical writers are not directly referring to preservation, the application is obvious: The Word of God which endures forever has been recorded in written form; therefore we can conclude that the written form (i.e., the Scriptures) will endure forever. This endurance is preservation.

One of the strongest additional proofs lies in the conservative's view of inspiration and inerrancy. If God chose to record His words to man without error in the original manuscripts, then it follows that He will also preserve them. If He did not preserve them, there would have been little reason for having an inerrant original.

II

THE PRESERVATION OF THE OLD TESTAMENT TEXT

It has been shown in the previous chapter that the Scriptures teach that God will preserve His Word. In the present chapter it will be demonstrated that God has indeed miraculously and providentially preserved the Old Testament text throughout history.

The History of the Preserved Text

The Text Prior to Ezra

The orthodox doctrine as set forth by the Westminster Confession states that the inspiration of the Scriptures extends to the original autographs only. The next step is to determine what constitutes the autographa. The obvious answer would seem to be that the autographa is what the author actually wrote himself. However, this is not necessarily always the case. The autographa of the Pentateuch especially needs defining because of the problems involved.

There are those who believe that Moses wrote or dictated every word in the Pentateuch. Such an interpretation has very serious problems. Deuteronomy 34 records in detail Moses' death and burial. Men like Philo and Josephus have defended the position that Moses was writing prophetically of his own death. This is unlikely, however, since it comes at the end of the Pentateuch and was written as a historical event. Allis suggests that many liberal theologians were so sure Moses did not write chapter 34 that they appended it to the book of Joshua.[25] It is likely that someone else wrote the final chapter of Deuteronomy without any attempt to identify himself.

The most common conservative position is that Moses or his amanuensis, using existing sources, wrote the Pentateuch during his life, and that copy was the autograph and inspired. Any later additions were not inspired but were merely scribal glosses trying to clarify terms which were becoming obsolete. These glosses may be true and correct but were not written as inspired of God.

Other conservatives feel that this definition of the autographa is not broad enough and causes many problems.

One of the problems seems to stem from the modernization of place names, locations of cities, and rivers. If these place names and locations are not inspired, it then becomes the task of the biblicist to determine what is the original autograph. This is the constant task of the textual critic. However, since the original copies are not extant it is impossible to determine the original reading because our current extant manuscripts have these modernizations in them.

The problem is in determining what terms were modernized and what were not. The task set before the textual critic is nearly impossible. He would have to deal with terms which are in our oldest extant manuscripts. But the only reason it is known that there are some modernizations of terms has been through the findings of archeology. Such findings have not been very numerous, but if there were more findings, perhaps other terms would prove to be modern terms of older names. It could conceivably create problems in our current understanding of geography.

Genesis 14 has a number of these scribal glosses. These glosses are in all of our existing manuscripts and are not copyist additons or corrections. The copyist glosses are a matter of textual criticism, whereas the scribal glosses of Genesis 14 appear in all extant manuscripts. Genesis 14:3 reads: "All these joined together in the vale of Siddim (the same is the Salt Sea)." The information in parentheses defines Siddim, since later in history this was obscure to the readers. The scribe who modernized or edited the text put the explanation in so as to make the text intelligible. In Genesis 11:31 the phrase "Ur of the Chaldees" appears. It is known from archeology that the Chaldeans did not come into existence until long after Abraham's time.[26] It is understood, then, that this is a scribal gloss for the benefit of later readers; otherwise, Ur may never have been identified because it was completely destroyed in later years. But it is consistent with God's character to give this added explanation through a redactor in order that the meaning of the text might not become obscure.

The view which holds to the expanded autographa of the Pentateuch is clearly stated by Pfeiffer when he writes:

The recognition of the Mosaic authorship of the Pentateuch does not deny the possibility, or even the probability of later editorial revision. Place names may be modernized in order to make them intelligible to a later generation. Joshua, the minister and successor of Moses, may have written the account of Moses' death recorded in the last chapter of Deuteronomy.[27]

Robert Dick Wilson, recognized as one of the most outstanding Old Testament scholars of modern times, writes:

> The Pentateuch as it stands is historical and from the time of Moses; and that Moses was its real author, though it may have been revised and edited by later redactors, the additions being just as much inspired and as true as the rest.[28]

Merrill F. Unger, another advocate of the expanded view of the autographa of the Pentateuch, writes:

> The Mosaic unity of the Pentateuch, moreover, does not necessarily preclude the possibility of later redactions of the whole work, so as to render it imperative to hold that Moses wrote with his own hand or dictated to amanuenses all and everything contained in it.[29]

Those who hold the view of a larger definition of the autographa feel that the true autographa is the finished work of the Pentateuch. A redactor, under the inspiration of the Holy Spirit, modernized the place names and text of the Hebrew.

Another reason for believing that the revisions were inspired is due to the evolution of the language. Evolution occurs in all languages. The King James Version of 1611 is very difficult to read in its original form. The King James Bible which is commonly read today resembles the original copies only remotely. Other early literary works written in English are also very difficult to understand today. The Elizabethan Age poem "Cuckoo Song" is virtually unreadable to those of the present day. It reads:

> Summer is icumen in:
> Lhude sing cucu!

Groweth sed, and bloweth med,
and springth the wude nu —
Sing cuccu!
Awe bleteth after lomb;
Lhouth after calve cu;
Balluc sterteth bucke verteth,
Murie sing cuccu!
Cuccu, cuccu, well singes thus, cuccu:
Ne swike thu naver nu.
Sing cuccu, nu, sing cuccu!
Sing cuccu, sing cuccu, nu![30]

The Hebrew language also has evolved. The English example represents five hundred to eight hundred years, whereas the Hebrew of the Pentateuch covers about thirty-five hundred years. The development of the Hebrew language at the time of Moses indicates that Moses did at least write in an alphabetic form.[31] Until about 200 B.C. the Hebrews used the form of the letters which are found in the Phoenician inscriptions. These letters were of an angular shape. The same form of letters is found in some of the earlier Hebrew finds such as the Siloam inscription, Moabite stone, and other inscriptions in dialects of Canaanite.[32]

Because of the great difference between the script of the Pentateuch and the script of the present-day text it became necessary that by Divine preservation God secured the accuracy of the text when changing from the Old Hebrew to the square characters.

The fact that it is not known who the redactors were or when these redactions took place should not cause alarm. For instance, many of the Old Testament books are anonymous and undatable, and yet their authenticity is not questioned by conservative scholars. It is consistent with God's purpose to enable readers thirty-five hundred years after the writing of the Pentateuch, to have a readable and understandable copy of the original manuscripts. It appears that such an inspired editing is necessary to maintain a pure, understandable text on which the reader can rely. Allis believes this final editing of the Pentateuch was completed by the fifth century B.C., before the succession of the prophets had ceased.[33]

Christians who maintain that God has miraculously

preserved His written Word have often overlooked the fact that if the glosses are not inspired then there may be much of the Old Testament which is not part of the original revelation, and yet appears in our extant manuscripts. The obvious explanation is that the modernization of the place-names in the Pentateuch were inspired and have been Divinely preserved throughout history.

The text of the period prior to Ezra was in a Samaritan script and developed until the square script took its place. It may have been Ezra who inserted the inspired glosses. It seems he would best qualify, since he authored one or more books of the Old Testament and would be the logical choice of God. It is doubtful, however, that Ezra was responsible for the change from the Old Hebrew text to the square script. The change probably came about during a later period.

The Text of the Sopherim Period (400 B.C.-A.D. 200)

The Sopherim were an order of scribes that began under Ezra. It was their responsibility to transmit the sacred Scriptures. Their major achievement was to standardize a pure text of the Hebrew Scriptures insofar as their manuscript sources permitted.[34]

Green writes:

> It was their function, as they understood and expressed it, "to put a hedge about the law," i.e., to ascertain, defend, and perpetuate the true interpretation of Scripture, and to preserve it from any possible error in transmission.[35]

The Sopherim began the formation of the critical observations on the text known as the Masora. These observations were enlarged on later by the Masoretes.[36] They counted the number of letters, words, and phrases, and the numbers of these different countings were placed at the end of each book. This enabled any scribe who was copying the Scriptures to check himself. After completing his job of transcribing a book he merely had to count the number of words, letters, and phrases to see if he had made a mistake. Archer points out: "It should be clearly understood that the Sopherim worked only with the consonantal text; they had nothing to do with the vowel points."[37]

It was perhaps during this period that the text was changed from Old Hebrew to the square script. Green writes:

> In this period occurred the change from the old to the more modern form of the Hebrew letter, not by the sudden introduction of a new character from abroad, but by gradual modification largely induced by the effort after regularity and symmetry of form and an elegant calligraphy befitting the sacred task in which the copyists were engaged. There is no reason to believe that this gradual alteration in the shape of the letters had any effect whatever upon the substance of the text.

The Text in the Masoretic Period (A.D. 500-950)

It was the Masoretes who gave the final form to the Hebrew text. They received the text from the Talmudic period and inserted an intricate vowel system which gave to each word the exact pronunciation and grammatical form. Their system allowed for a certain amount of textual criticism. Whenever they suspected the word indicated by the consonantal text to be incorrect, they corrected it by inserting in very small letters in the margin the vowel points which belonged to the correct word.[38]

The Masoretes had one objective in mind, as Unger puts it: "to determine the exact text handed down to them from all available evidence and to hand it on to future generations without change."[39] They accomplished their goal with amazing accuracy.

When the Masoretes were faced with a decision as to what reading was the true one, they did not pick one reading and cast out the other. Instead they preserved the most likely in the text; the other they placed in the margin. The *Kethiv* was the reading in the consonantal text, but on it were placed the vowel signs that did not fit it, which were to be read with consonants of the preferred marginal reading which was called the *Qere*.

When the Masoretic text was finally established, the previous existing manuscripts were placed in the *genizoth*. The final recension of the Masoretic text became the standard for all subsequent copies. All the extant Hebrew manuscripts are based on the Masoretic text. This is the reason that there is so little variation in our extant manuscripts. Unger speaks highly of the Masoretic tradition:

> This text, moreover, in the light of the phenomenal labors of the Masoretic scholars and their loyal devotion to traditional readings and to the Scriptures as the revered, inspired Word of God, inviolable and holy, may be considered as a faithful reproduction not only of the text of about A.D. 90, but of the autographic copies themselves.[40]

Green likewise writes:

> The sum of the whole matter is this: The Hebrew manuscripts cannot compare with those of the New Testament either in antiquity or number, but they have been written with greater care and exhibit fewer various readings obtained from an extensive collation of the Hebrew manuscripts. They are of little importance, for they all represent substantially what is known as the Masoretic text. This is so minutely guarded by the Masora, that it can by its aid be accurately determined, and traced back long prior to existing manuscripts.[41]

Thus, the text of the Old Testament has been Divinely preserved from the autographa to the present day. God has chosen the Old Testament to be preserved through the traditional Masoretic text which was faithfully preserved by the scribes and priests (Rom. 3:2). Hills, writing concerning the Masoretic text, says, "Thus it was that the Hebrew Old Testament text, Divinely inspired and providentially preserved, was restored to the church and the promise of Christ was fulfilled."[42]

The Place of Textual Criticism

The first step in textual criticism is to establish the traditional text, which is referred to as the Masoretic text. There are certain general rules which must be established in determining what the correct traditional text is. Even though the variants are few and minor, the correct text must be established.

It is generally agreed among conservative textual critics

that where the Masoretic text is unobjectionable in subject material and language it is preferred above all other texts such as the Septuagint version, Samaritan Pentateuch, Targums, Peshitta, and Latin Vulgate.

Evidence That the Text Has Been Preserved

An examination of the Hebrew manuscripts now in existence shows that in the whole Old Testament there are scarcely any variants supported by more than one manuscript out of two hundred to four hundred, in which each book is found, except in the use of the full and defective writing of the vowels.[43]

The variants gathered from the Masorites number about twelve hundred. The various Aramaic versions, the Syriac Peshitto, the Samaritan version, and the Latin Vulgate, but for slight variations, agree with the present text. These variants include letters or proper names, variations due to sound, variants in gutturals, and vowel pointing. Most of the large number of variants are very unimportant.[44]

It must be remembered that whereas the Masoretic text has maintained a unity in transmission, the Septuagint manuscripts differ widely even centuries later. Wurthwein writes, "But even those who disagree with him [referring to Kahle's disagreement with Lagarde] must admit that we are today still very far from an original text which can be set over against M as a unified whole." Unger's evaluation of the weakness of the Septuagint indicates that it cannot be as important as the traditional text:

The critical value of the Septuagint, on the other hand, despite the antiquity of its witness to the Hebrew text, is substantially reduced, as noted, because the translation varies in its standard of excellence and in its precise purpose, is conditioned by peculiar difficulties, manifests both a loyalty and a freedom in dealing with the original and is marred by a large number of inaccuracies and mistakes. Added to this, there is no homogeneous extant text. Septuaginal manuscripts become exceedingly corrupt in the course of transmission and it is now evidently impossible to recapture completely the original text.[45]

Wilson lists the variations, such as differences in point-ing, errors of sight, sound, differences in interpretation of abbreviations, transpositions, additions, or omissions, and so forth, but sums it up by stating, "The result of his investigation [R. H. Charles's] is a wonderful corrobora-tion of the substantial correctness of our present Hebrew text."[46]

The Samaritan Pentateuch in Hebrew agrees sub-stantially with the Masoretic text. Most of the variations are of the same character as those prevalent in the trans-mission of all originals.[47]

The Dead Sea Scrolls also give remarkable evidence of the preservation of the Hebrew text which we now possess. Burrows, who is no friend to the conservative, writes:

> Many of the differences between the St. Mark's Isaiah scroll and the Masoretic text can be explained as mistakes in copying. Apart from these, there is a remarkable agreement, on the whole, with the text found in the medieval manuscripts. Such agreement in a manuscript so much older gives reassuring testi-mony to the general accuracy of the traditional text. . . . What it shows is that any major changes that occurred in the transmission of the text had already been made before the beginning of the Christian era. . . .
>
> Herein lies its chief importance, supporting the fidelity of the Masoretic tradition.[48]

Not only in general can it be stated that the manuscripts vary only a little, but in minute details it can be demon-strated that our text has been Divinely preserved.

Wilson has compiled a number of specific instances in which the text can be demonstrated to be accurate in details during transmission. There were twenty-six or more foreign kings whose names have been found on documents which were contemporary with the kings. The spelling of many of these names coincides with the spelling in the Old Testament. In some of the spellings in which there were differences it is in accordance with the laws of phonetic change as those laws were in operation at the time when the documents were written. In no case can the spelling in our Hebrew text be demonstrated to be in error.[49]

It has also been found that many names of the kings of Israel and Judah as found in contemporary Assyrian documents likewise agree in spelling with our Old Testament. Wilson sums it up in this way:

> Thus we find that in 143 cases of transliteration from Egyptian, Assyrian, Babylonian, and Moabite into Hebrew and in forty cases of the opposite, or 184 in all [143 + 40 = 183, not 184], the evidence shows that for twenty-three hundred to thirty-nine hundred years the text of the proper names in the Hebrew Bible has been transmitted with the most minute accuracy.... Further, that the Hebrew text should have been transmitted by copyists through so many centuries is a phenomenon unequalled in the history of literature.

Such accuracy in the transmitting of proper names is very difficult. This can be demonstrated in several instances. In the life of Alexander by the Pseudo-Callisthenes, a daughter-in-law of Queen Candace is called Harpussa twice, Matersa another, and Margie once more. In a list of combatants in the games, the Syriac has nine names like the Greek and Latin authorities, but they have been altered to the extent that only two or three have any resemblance.[50]

Wilson further argues that since it can be demonstrated that the spelling of proper names of kings as given in the Old Testament is correct, the spelling must go back to the original sources; and if the original sources were in the hands of the writers of the documents, the probability is very great that since the writers were correct in their spelling of the names of the kings they were also correct in recording the deeds about the kings. This is what has been found in general to be true where the Hebrew documents and the monuments both record the great deeds of the kings.[51]

Out of fifty-six kings of Egypt from Shishak to Darius II and out of the numerous kings of Assyria, Babylon, Persia, Tyre, Damascus, Moab, Israel, and Judah, who ruled from 2000 to 400 B.C., the writers of the Old Testament have put forty or more that are mentioned in records of two or more of the nations, in proper chronological order with respect to kings of other countries and of the same country. Wilson concludes that "no stronger evidence for the substantial accuracy of the Old Testament records could possibly be imagined than this collection of names and kings."[52]

Skilton has summed up the matter very well: "And we can be grateful that, along with our Hebrew texts, the care and providence of God have provided versions and other aids for the important and necessary work of textual criticism."[53]

The preservation of the Old Testament has been primarily fulfilled in the form of the Masoretic text. Not any Masoretic manuscript possesses the pure text, but all of God's words which He recorded in the autographs are present in our extant manuscripts.

It has been shown in this chapter that God has Divinely preserved His Word throughout history. He provided for modernization of place names and changes in the form of the letters by having the text edited under inspiration sometime around the fourth or fifth century B.C.

III

THE PRESERVATION OF THE NEW TESTAMENT

The Traditional Text

The Traditional Text Defined

The Traditional Text of the New Testament has been known by several designations. The most common designation is *Textus Receptus;* others have called it the Byzantine Text. Although both of these names are descriptive of the Traditional Text they still lack complete accuracy. The term *Textus Receptus* was derived from the preface of the text produced by Bonaventure and Abraham Elzevir in 1633. In their preface they made the assertion: *"textum ergo habes, nunc ab omnibus receptum"* (therefore you have a text now received by all). From this came the name *Textus Receptus* (Received Text).[54]

The term Byzantine Text has certain negative connotations. The Byzantine Text is often erroneously associated with a local text produced at Constantinople that does not represent the true New Testament text. With such associations, the term is obviously undesirable.

It must be kept in mind that there is no definitive edition of the *Textus Receptus*. There are more than twenty-five editions, each varying slightly from the other. It is based on late manuscripts and was produced by uncritical methods. Nevertheless, even though there are slight variations, the text displays a distinct textual character.[55] This text-form is found in the vast majority of all extant Greek manuscripts. Hodges explains the reason for the resemblance between the great majority of texts and the *Textus Receptus*, despite the uncritical methodology of its compilation, when he writes:

> The textual tradition found in Greek manuscripts is for the most part so uniform that to select out of the mass of witnesses almost any manuscript at random is to select a manuscript likely to be very much like most other manuscripts. Thus, when our printed editions were made, the odds favored their early editors coming across manuscripts exhibiting this majority text.... Accordingly, the TR represents a form of text most closely akin to the form which prevails in the Greek manuscript tradition as a whole.[56]

Since the Traditional Text is not to be found in any one edition of the *Textus Receptus* and since the designation Byzantine Text implies that the Traditional Text may be only a local text, the best title to designate the Traditional Text is the "Majority Text." Our editions of the *Textus Receptus* need to be critically compared with the majority of manuscripts to determine what is exactly the Majority Text.

The Traditional Text in Its Earliest Form

The books of the New Testament were originally written in Greek, which was the common language of nearly all the territories that made up the eastern half of the Roman world. It was for these people that the Gospels and the Epistles were originally written. Shortly after their production many hand-copied manuscripts were reproduced. These manuscripts were for churches, individuals who could afford them, or for libraries. Copies were made of the copies, and then those were copied. It was not long before translations were made from the copies also.

Almost immediately errors began to appear in the copies. Such errors as spelling changes and omissions were natural errors of the scribes when they became tired or careless. When a copy having mistakes was compared with others, the mistakes were clearly revealed and easily corrected. Heretics also arose early who tampered with the text to make it conform to their own error. The outcome was that erroneous copies of the New Testament began to circulate.

There were also men with good intentions who attempted to supply conjectural emendations instead of correcting defects by comparing readings with other manuscripts.

The Traditional Text was prominent in the second and third centuries and had become dominant in the Greek-speaking churches by the end of the fourth century. By now scribes were on guard for defective copies. When copies were found which had been corrupted, they were taken out of circulation or destroyed. This may have been the case with Codex B and Aleph. Perhaps scribes detected their impurity and took them out of circulation. This enabled them to be preserved for a great number of years without much deterioration. Pure copies of the manuscripts would have been worn out through use, and for this reason we have only late extant manuscripts of the Majority Text.

The Traditional Text in Western Europe

Contrary to the eastern section of the Roman Empire, the western division knew very little Greek. Their language was Latin, which they had received from their conquerors. In this area the earlier translations of the Greek into Latin finally gave way to the Latin Vulgate (342-420). Christians became organized into the Roman Catholic Church ruled by the pope. From this time until the tenth century learning was hampered by the invasion of the barbarians. This period is known as the Dark Ages in history.[57]

The Vulgate had little practical value to the common man, since he could understand very little of it. Because of the low standard of education and carelessness of the monkist scribes, the text became corrupt. But by the fourteenth century there were signs that Europe was awakening from its intellectual slumber. Wycliffe was among the first to realize the importance of Bible translation into the vernacular. He translated the Latin Bible into English with a great deal of success.[58]

The Traditional Text in the Byzantine Empire

The Emperor Diocletian in the third century divided the Roman Empire into the eastern and western empires. Then, when Constantine became a strong political leader, an edict was issued granting toleration to the practice of Christianity. Later he professed Christianity and encouraged others to follow his example. In 324 he became sole ruler of the empire. In 330 he left Rome and rebuilt Byzantium and renamed it after himself, Constantinople. Then, in 395 the permanent division was made between the eastern and western empires. Constantinople naturally became the center of culture and headquarters for Greek-speaking Christians under the organization of the Greek Orthodox Church.[59]

For the first three hundred years, and especially during the reign of Justinian I (527-565), the Byzantine Empire was the greatest power on earth. In the seventh century the Moslems began to take some of the power from the Byzantine Empire, which continued through the following centuries. In the thirteenth century the Islamic Ottoman Turks began to move into the plains of Central Asia. They captured the Arab territories and advanced into Asia Minor itself.[60] In 1453 Constantinople was invaded by these Moslems and fell prey to its hordes. This started the flight of the Greek scholars and Christians into Europe with their Greek New Testament manuscripts.

The Greek grammars which the Christians brought with them from Constantinople were all based on the original work of Dionysius Thrax, which had been produced in Alexandria more than fifteen hundred years earlier. These were the same grammars which were used by the men who produced the first Greek New Testaments.[61] Hills writes, "Thus the providence of God not only preserved intact the Greek New Testament text but also kept in continual existence the language in which it was written."[62]

The Traditional Text Standardized

At the turn of the sixteenth century the Renaissance was in full swing in Italy and was influencing the entire continent of Europe. The Renaissance came about because of "long periods of peace, abundant wealth, knowledge obtained by travel and observation, a large leisure class; and the consequent cultivation of the mental powers which has always followed such conditions."[63] The Renaissance enabled men to substitute a modern secular approach to life for a medieval religious life.

Desiderius Erasmus of Rotterdam was born and educated in this new era of thinking. The emphasis on ancient Greek and pre-Christian sources enabled him to become well educated in Greek. With his interest in the Scriptures, he became a very qualified and able man to provide Christendom with its first Greek Testament.

Although Erasmus' edition of the New Testament was the first published, it was not the first printed; that honor belongs to Francis Ximenes de Cisneros, Archbishop of Toledo. In 1502 Ximenes in honor of Emperor Charles V began the *Complutensian Polyglott*. It contained the entire Bible, the Old Testament in Hebrew, Greek, and Latin, the New Testament in Greek and Latin.[64] The volume including the New Testament produced by Ximenes was completed January 10, 1514, two years prior to Erasmus' edition. The publication was delayed until the Old Testament would be ready to accompany it. It occupied four volumes and was completed July 10, 1517. It was not authorized for publication by Leo X, however, until March 22, 1520; and it was not actually issued until 1522.[65]

Kenyon points out that the preface and dedication to the text state that the text was derived from manuscripts loaned by Leo X from the Vatican Library. The editors indicate that they used the best possible manuscripts available, which may imply they exercised some selection and critical judgment.[66] There is no evidence that manuscript B was used.

This edition appears to have been a very scholarly piece of work; however, it never gained much acceptance, probably due to the fact that Erasmus' edition had perhaps six years' head start. Also, the Polyglott consisted of six volumes, which were quite expensive, whereas Erasmus' edition was in one volume and cost comparatively little, giving it a greater circulation.

Erasmus had planned for several years to produce a
Greek text, but the rumor that the Polyglott was going to
be published may have hastened the plan for completing
his text. A Swiss printer, Froben, sought out Erasmus in
April 1515 and asked him to prepare as quickly as possible
a Greek New Testament. Since Erasmus had been anxious
to do it anyway, he set out willingly in September 1515.[67]
It was completed and published only seven months later, in
March 1516, under the title, *"Novum instrumentum omne,
deligenter ab Erasmo Rot. recognitum it emendotum"* and
dedicated to Leo X.

For his first edition, Erasmus had only ten manuscripts:
four from England, five at Basle, and one loaned to him by
John Reuchlin. The latter manuscript seemed old enough
to Erasmus to have been from the apostolic age but is
usually assigned by modern critics to be from the tenth or
twelfth century. It was from this manuscript that he
produced the Book of Revelation. One of the best manuscripts of the Basle collection, he felt, was altered to agree
with the Vulgate. He took nearly all the Gospels from a
cursive manuscript of about the fifteenth century or a
little earlier. For Acts and the epistles he used older manuscripts, some of which he never bothered to copy but
merely made chalk corrections in red.

The first edition has been ridiculed by modern scholars,
and perhaps with a great deal of justification; however, it
must be pointed out that Erasmus did actually collate
manuscripts on critical principles of sorts. By means of
grammatical and historical knowledge he produced
superior readings in some places to the texts of his contemporaries. And he also compared citations from the Old
Testament with the Septuagint.

Erasmus did not leave his critical work with the success-
ful publication in 1516. In his second edition in 1519 he
introduced four hundred alterations.[68] He used additional
manuscripts, including a Latin manuscript, Codex Aureus,
loaned to him by the king of Hungary; two manuscripts
from the Austin Priory or Corsendonk; and a Greek manuscript borrowed from the Monastery of Mount St.
Agnes.[69]

A third edition was produced in 1522, which has been
famous for the *"comma Johanneum."* In 1520-21, while in

Brussels, Erasmus consulted two old manuscripts at the library of St. Donation, dated in the fourteenth century. In this text, in I John 5:7, appeared the phrase, "For there are three that bear record in heaven, the Father, the Word, and the Holy Ghost and these three are one." Erasmus was unable to find the text in any Greek manuscript so he decided to omit it. He was attacked by his contemporaries. Kenyon describes the controversy:

> In controversy with Stunica, Erasmus had promised to insert it if any Greek MS could be produced in which it occurred. It was found (in a clumsy form) in a MS in England (Evan. 61, now at Dublin), and Erasmus, though rightly supposing that it was due merely to retranslation from the Latin, inserted it in fulfillment of his promise. Hence the passage (for which there is early Latin authority) found its way into the *Textus Receptus.*[70]

Erasmus produced two more editions: one in 1527, in which he made use of the Complutension edition, and one in 1535, which differs very little from the previous edition.

Attacks on the Traditional Text

In the 1860s the Codex Sinaiticus and the Codex Vaticanus became available to New Testament textual critics. In 1881 Westcott and Hort published a two-volume work, *The New Testament in the Original Greek,* in which they advanced a theory that the true New Testament text was to be found in the text represented in these two fourth century manuscripts. These manuscripts are also the basis of the Nestle text and many of the modern translations of the English Bible.

The Claim That the Majority Text Is a Revised Ecclesiastical Text

Westcott and Hort believed that some time between A.D. 250 and 350 an effort was made to revise and standardize the widely conflicting manuscript tradition of the time. From this revision emerged a form of text which gained a predominance over all other text forms.[71] This text type was called the Syrian text by Westcott and Hort. Later scholars identified the Syrian text with the term

"Byzantine." Greenlee writes describing Hort's view:

> After Christianity attained official status in the
> fourth century, attempts began to be made, officially
> or unofficially, to deal with the divergencies in the
> text, aiming at combining readings where appropriate,
> removing obscurities, harmonizing parallels, and in
> general to produce a smooth text free from diffi-
> culties. Thus arose the "Syrian" text, which was
> smooth and sensible, yet lacking in the vigor and
> occasional ruggedness of the original.[72]

Many modern textual critics say, then, that the Majority
Text is an ecclesiastical text and far inferior to the text
exhibited, in Codex Vaticanus and Sinaiticus. Hodges
writes: "Hence, so the argument runs, the very fact of
revision, especially an eclectic revision of this kind,
necessarily reduces the testimony of this majority of
manuscripts to a secondary level."[73] The older manuscripts are then preferred; and even if they were revised, it
was supposedly much less than has been exhibited in the
Majority Text.

The view presented by Westcott and Hort, of an
authoritative ecclesiastical revision (i.e., the origin of the
Syrian text), has widely been abandoned. Colwell writes
concerning the deficiency of this view:

> Many years ago I joined others in pointing out the
> limitations in Hort's use of genealogy, and the
> inapplicability of genealogical method—strictly
> defined—to the textual criticism of the N.T. Since
> then many others have assented to this criticism, and
> the building of family trees is only rarely
> attempted.[74]

Aland also writes of its failure:

> For, the increase of the documentary evidence and
> the entirely new areas of research which opened to
> use on the discovery of the papyri, mean the end of
> Westcott and Hort's conception [referring to the
> different recensions and text types]. We can no
> longer take their conception as valid, as long as its

raison d'être, even under the new conditions, has not been proved.[75]

Nevertheless it was this theory that gave an inferior status to the Majority Text and hence opportunities for more attacks on it.

These modern textual critics are not agreed among themselves as to the origin of the Majority Text, but are generally agreed that the oldest manuscripts are more reliable than those on which the *Textus Receptus* is based. Nevertheless, because of the textual work of Westcott and Hort, any straw is sought after in order to dethrone the *Textus Receptus;* hence another theory is devised to account for the origin of the Majority Text representing 85 to 90 percent of all extant manuscripts.

The major weakness of such a theory is that its basis is purely subjective. The view stems from the Westcott and Hort theory but is more subjective. Hodges points out its weakness when he writes:

No one has yet explained how a long, slow process spread out over many centuries as well as over a wide geographical area, and involving a multitude of copyists who often knew nothing of the state of the text outside of their own monasteries or scriptoria, could achieve this widespread uniformity out of the diversity presented by the earliest forms of text. Even an official edition of the New Testament—promoted with ecclesiastical sanction throughout the known world—would have had great difficulty achieving this result, as the history of Jerome's Vulgate amply demonstrates. But an unguided process achieving relative stability and uniformity in the diversified textual, historical, and cultural circumstances in which the New Testament was copied, imposes impossible strains on our imagination.[76]

The theory of a smooth text immediately finds appeal to most people. One can casually compare the readings of the critical text (usually Nestle's) with those of the *Textus Receptus* and it becomes apparent at once that the *Textus Receptus* has the smoothest reading. The theory often stated is that the scribes had a tendency to smooth out the text to make it clearer or to produce a better rendering; hence came the *Textus Receptus* and its expanded readings.

The Claim That the Majority Text Is Based on Late Manuscripts and Therefore Unreliable

The fact that there are no extant Greek manuscripts which support the Majority Text prior to the fourth century is perhaps the strongest claim in favor of the superiority of the text form of Codex Sinaiticus and Codex Vaticanus. This is strengthened by the recent discovery of manuscripts which support the critical text (i.e., the text form of Sinaiticus and Vaticanus) which date around A.D. 200.

As convincing as this may seem, the fact still remains that the oldest manuscript does not necessarily contain the best text. Aland, a proponent of the critical text, writes, "P-47 is, for example, by far the oldest of the manuscripts containing the full or almost full text of the Apocalypse; but it is certainly not the best."[77]

It has been pointed out that all of the most ancient manuscripts which we now possess have come from Egypt. The climate in that part of the world lends itself to the preservation of manuscripts. There is no good evidence to suppose that these manuscripts represent the same text which was known in the other parts of the world.

There is strong logical evidence that the majority of manuscripts best represent the original rather than a few older manuscripts. This is stated very well by Hodges:

Under normal circumstances the older a text is than its rivals, the greater are its chances to survive in a plurality or a majority of the texts extant at any subsequent period. But the oldest text of all is the autograph. Thus it ought to be taken for granted that, barring some radical dislocation in the history of transmission, a majority of texts will be far more likely to represent correctly the character of the original than a small minority of texts. This is especially true when the ratio is an overwhelming 9:1.

Under any reasonable normal transmissional conditions, it would be for all practical purposes quite impossible for a later text form to secure so one-sided a preponderance of extant witnesses. Even if we push the origination of the so-called Byzantine text back to a date coeval with P-75 and P-66 (ca. 200), a time when already there must have been hundreds of manuscripts in existence, such mathematical proportions as the surviving tradition reveals could not be accounted for apart from some prodigious upheaval in textual history.[78]

Evidence for the Majority Text

Today there are about 5,255 extant manuscripts: 81 Papyri; 267 Majuscules; 2,764 Minuscules; 2,143 Lexionaries.[79] Of these manuscripts, the overwhelming majority—somewhere between 80 and 90 percent—support the Traditional Text. Hodges writes:

> It is also well known among students of textual criticism that a large majority of this huge mass of manuscripts—somewhere between 80-90 percent—contain a Greek text which in most respects closely resembles the kind of text which was the basis of our King James Version.[80]

Method of Textual Criticism

The Method of Current Critical Scholars

The basic method of textual criticism for those who view the original text as lying under the old manuscripts (A, B, Aleph, C, D) is essentially subjective. They believe that the true text of the New Testament is represented by one or more of these manuscripts. A great deal of significance is placed on these five manuscripts—and especially on B and Aleph—even though the five are never in exact accord.[81] Burgon writes:

> They seem to base their claim on "antiquity"; but the real confidence of many of them lies evidently in a claim to subtle divination, which enables them to recognize a true reading on the true text when they see it. Strange, that it does not seem to have struck such critics that they assume the very thing which has to be proved.[82]

To many, the thought of subjective judgment has a ring of authenticity. It may sound good, but it is weak. Each student who reads a text may have a completely different understanding of the passage. He may choose the reading others feel to be completely foreign to the context. But in practice, the internal evidence is often what critics lean on most to determine a particular reading, especially if the manuscripts are somewhat divided. An example of this is the printed editions of the Greek New Testament. If one would compare the texts of Nestle, Westcott and Hort, Tischendorf, Merk, and the American Bible Society, the variants would be overwhelming.

When a student turns to any one of these modern Greek texts he cannot possibly say that this is the Word of God. The men producing the modern texts do not even claim to have the correct text. The editors of the United Bible Society Greek Text write, "It is the intention of the Committee from time to time to revise its work in order to take into account new discoveries and fresh evidence."[83]

Hodges points out the weakness of the subjective method of criticism:

> For then every man's judgment would be theoretically as valid as every other man's. The text would then be either quite uncertain or would rest (as in fact it does in modern critical editions) upon a consensus of contemporary scholars. Granted some minds feel safer when holding to a popular, majority view. But this is a poor substitute for evidence, and the history of human thought proves it to be most uncertain. Today's consensus is too frequently tomorrow's curiosity.

> But, in the final analysis, subjectivism is a retreat from the hard and demanding task of original thought and research. Conservatives who give way to eclecticism and subjectivism, instead of rising to the challenge of fresh, original work, deserve to be left behind by the moving stream of events.[84]

The Method of Obtaining the Majority Text

Since I hold that the true text can be found in the Majority Text, in order to determine what this is one must count the number of manuscripts of any given reading. This method has been bitterly criticized because it does not consider the age of manuscripts. But as was discussed earlier, the readings supported by the preponderance of manuscripts is more likely to be the original text. Since the original text is the oldest, it is reasonable that the largest number of manuscripts would best represent the original. If the percentage were close, then the number of manuscripts would not be so significant; but since the Majority Text represents from 80 to 90 percent, it is significant.

An edition of the Greek New Testament with a critical apparatus representing all the known manuscript readings is impossible at the present time. Out of the over fifty-two hundred extant manuscripts, only a fraction of these have been collated. There is now an attempt to collate many more minuscule manuscripts by the *Institut Fur Neutestamantliche Textforschung.* When this study is complete there will be much more material available to witness to the Majority Text. At the present the work of Hermann von Soden[85] is the major source of information. Von Soden's work is not, however, without its problems. One cannot be certain in many cases just how adequate his judgments have been. One simply cannot be sure the apparatus can be trusted to record the facts accurately. Nevertheless von Soden is an indispensable tool for determining the Majority Text. By counting the manuscripts in his K (Majority Text) and I (Independent Text, represented in Nestle by pm) texts, one can come to the majority reading.

This method emphasizes an objective standard by which we may obtain the true text. Although there are variants within the *Textus Receptus* these are extremely few and often trivial, which demonstrates the highly stable character of the manuscript tradition.

Hodges sums up the matter:

> It remains to add only one point. When the history of the New Testament text is interpreted in this way (the Majority Text being the superior text), the widespread uniformity of the manuscripts at once becomes a potent tribute to the providence of God in preserving His Word. There is no other interpretation of textual history that can make this claim without

serious reservations. For if the mass of witnesses is corrupt, 90 percent of the tradition is corrupt. And no one is quite sure how to use the remaining 10 percent![86]

IV

CONCLUSION

Preservation of the Scriptures is both a doctrine and a dogma, because its basis is both found in the Scriptures and has been included in major confessions throughout ecclesiastical history. The question is: What is guaranteed by the doctrine of preservation? Has God preserved His Word so that merely none of His Word which affects the most important doctrinal matters has perished? Or has God providentially preserved within the manuscript tradition every word which He spoke through the Scriptures?

I have defended the thesis that the Scriptures teach and history has proved that God has preserved every word of His written revelation, not in any one manuscript, but dispersed throughout the manuscript tradition.

The Old Testament is unique in its history of preservation. The Pentateuch, for instance, was written about 1500 B.C. and yet, until the discovery of the Dead Sea Scrolls, the present extant manuscripts of the entire Old Testament were dated about the tenth century. Certain descriptions of geography and the script of Moses' day changed during the history of the language. And all of these unite to make the Old Testament a special problem for preservation. Yet God has sovereignly undertaken to preserve His Word through errant men. This was accomplished through various means. Scribes very early developed minute methods for preserving the text as it was transmitted. Other scribes with Divine guidance modernized the text. This (specifically in the Pentateuch) enabled later readers to identify various geographical locations which would have become unidentifiable. Hebrew script also had changed, and it became necessary for the Pentateuch to be placed in the new script in order to be read and preserved.

The New Testament, like the Old, faced many dangers. The number of manuscripts of the New Testament which are extant is staggering. There is no ancient document of secular origin which enjoys such overwhelming attestation. The problem is not whether or not we have the general teaching of the Scriptures but whether or not we have the very words.

There are two basic conservative opinions as to what is involved in preservation and what text best represents God's providential preservation. One of these I have called the "Critical Text" position and the other I have called the "Majority Text" position.

Those embracing the Critical Text position believe that God has preserved His Word with "essential purity" through a few manuscripts which exhibit a text several hundred years older than the Majority Text. Since the Critical Text position arose with the work of Westcott and Hort in the nineteenth century after the discovery of Aleph and B, they are saying in effect that the true text of the Scriptures of the New Testament remained unknown from the Byzantine period until the discovery of Aleph and B about a thousand years later. It must be said that they are not concerned that the true text was not known for nearly a thousand years.

I have shown that the Majority Text can be demonstrated to represent a tradition older than Aleph, B, and P-75 (A.D. 175-225). It has also been shown that there are Majority Text readings in extant manuscripts dating before Aleph and B. Such evidence is damaging to the scholars who follow Critical Text and who for many years maintained there were no Majority Text readings nearly as old as the readings in Aleph and B.

I have also pointed out that the theory of Westcott and Hort, which is actually responsible for dethroning the *Textus Receptus,* is no longer in good standing among modern textual critics. These same critics have not, however, found their way back to the superiority of the Majority Text, but have instead sought other explanations as to the origin of the Byzantine text—all of which seem woefully inadequate. As time goes on, textual critics are giving more and more weight to the Byzantine text. Some see it as neither a primary nor secondary text, but, at least, completely independent.[87]

It is my position that God has preserved His Word in an unbroken tradition as displayed in the Masoretic text of the Old Testament and the Majority Text of the New Testament. This position best corresponds to the Scripture's teaching that God's Word will endure forever. The Westminster Confession states the doctrine of preservation very well when it says:

> The Old Testament in Hebrew, and the New Testament in Greek, being immediately inspired by God, and, by His singular care and providence, kept pure in all ages, are therefore authentic; so as, in all controversies of religion, the Church is finally to appeal unto them.[8]

NOTES

[1]Carl F. H. Henry, "Inspiration," *Baker's Dictionary of Theology*, ed. Everett F. Harrison (Grand Rapids: Baker Book House, 1966), p. 286.

[2]Walter Rauschenbusch, *A Theology for the Social Gospel* (New York: The Macmillan Company, 1917), p. 194.

[3]*Sancti Irenaei Episcopi Lugdunensis et Martyris Detactionis et Eversionis Falso Cognominatae Agnitionis seu Contra Haereses Libra Quinque*. Part I, Vol. 7 of *Patrologiae Cursus Completus Series Graeca*, ed. J. P. Migne (n.p., 1857), 7, Col. 805. (Personal translation.)

[4]Augustine, cited by Thomas Cranmer, "Confutation of Unwritten Verities," *The Works of Thomas Cranmer*, ed. John Edmund Cox (2 vols.; Cambridge: The University Press, 1846), 2:33.

[5]John Calvin, *Institutes of the Christian Religion*, trans. John Allen (3 vols.; London: Printed for J. Walker; J. Hatchard; J. Richardson; L. B. Seeley; R. Baldwin; J. Black; Gale, Curtis, and Fenner; and Williams and Son, 1813), 1:80.

[6]John William Burgon, *The Traditional Text of the Holy Gospels Vindicated and Established*, arranged, completed and edited Edward Miller (London: George Bell and Sons, 1896), p. 12.

[7]Alfred Martin, "The Word of the Lord Endureth Forever," *Founders Week Messages 1966* (Chicago: Moody Bible Institute, 1966), p. 284.

[8]Burgon, *Traditional Text*, p. 12.

[9]S. W. Carruthers, *The Westminster Confession of Faith* (7th ed.; Manchester: R. Aikman and Son, n.d.), p. 92.

[10]"Formula Consensus Ecclesiarum Helveticarum Reformatarum," *Collectio Confessionum in Ecclesiis Reformatis Publicatarum*, ed. H. A. Niemeyer (Lipsiae: Sumptibus Iulii Klinkhardti, 1840), p. 730. (Personal translation.)

[11]Alfred Martin, "The Word of the Lord Endureth Forever," *Founder's Week Messages 1966* (Chicago: Moody Bible Institute, 1966), p. 284.

[12]Franz Delitzsch, *Biblical Commentary on the Psalms*, trans. Francis Bolton (3 vols.; Grand Rapids: Wm. B. Eerdmans Publishing Co., 1967), 3:254.

[13]Robert P. Lightner, *The Saviour and the Scriptures* (Philadelphia: Presbyterian and Reformed Publishing Co., 1966), p. 68.

[14]*Ibid.,* p. 61.

[15]Lewis Sperry Chafer, *Systematic Theology,* Vol. 1: *Prolegomena, Bibliology, and Theology Proper* (8 vols.; Dallas: Dallas Seminary Press, 1947), p. 121.

[16]Lightner, *Saviour,* p. 102.

[17]Edward J. Young, *Thy Word Is Truth* (Grand Rapids: Wm. B. Eerdmans Publishing Co., 1957), p. 27.

[18]William G. T. Shedd, *Dogmatic Theology* (3 vols.; Grand Rapids: Zondervan Publishing House, n.d.), 2:509.

[19]John H. Skilton, "The Transmission of the Scriptures," *The Infallible Word,* ed. N. B. Stonehouse and Paul Woolley (3d rev. ed.; Philadelphia: Presbyterian and Reformed Publishing Co., 1946), p. 143.

[20]*Ibid.*

[21]Edward F. Hills, *The King James Version Defended* (Des Moines: The Christian Research Press, 1956), pp. 24-25.

[22]Edward J. Young, *Thy Word Is Truth* (Grand Rapids: Wm. B. Eerdmans Co., 1957), p. 61.

[23]Skilton, "The Transmission," p. 143.

[24]Edward F. Hills, "Introduction," *The Last Twelve Verses of the Gospel According to St. Mark* by John W. Burgon (reprint of 1871 ed.; Evansville, Ind.: The Sovereign Grace Book Club, 1959), p. 37.

[25]Oswald T. Allis, *The Five Books of Moses* (Philadelphia: The Presbyterian and Reformed Publishing Co., 1964), pp. 12-13.

[26]Merrill F. Unger, "Introduction to the Old Testament 207" (unpublished class notes, Dallas Theological Seminary, Fall, 1966).

[27]Charles F. Pfeiffer, *The Book of Genesis* (Grand Rapids: Baker Book House, 1958), p. 7.

[28]Robert Dick Wilson, *A Scientific Investigation of the Old Testament* (Philadelphia: The Sunday School Times Co., 1926), p. 11.

[29]Merrill F. Unger, *Introductory Guide to the Old Testament* (Grand Rapids: Zondervan Publishing House, 1951), p. 238.

[30]Bernard D. Grebanier, Samuel Middlebrook, Stith Thompson, and William Watt, *English Literature and Its Backgrounds* (New York: Holt, Rinehart, and Winston, 1963), p. 65.

[31]F. F. Bruce, *The Books and the Parchments* (3d rev.; Old Tappan, N.J.: Fleming H. Revell Co., 1963), p. 30.

[32]*Ibid.,* p. 38.

[33]Allis, *Books of Moses,* p. 13.

[34]Gleason L. Archer, Jr., *A Survey of Old Testament Introduction* (Chicago: Moody Press, 1964), p. 54.

[35]William Henry Green, *General Introduction to the Old Testament: The Text* (New York: Charles Scribner's Sons, 1899), p. 146.

[36]*Ibid.,* p. 147.

[37]Archer, *Survey,* p. 54.

[38]*Ibid,* p. 56.

39Unger, *Introductory Guide,* p. 134.

40*Ibid.,* p. 137.

41Green, *General Introduction,* pp. 179-180.

42Edward F. Hills, *Believing Bible Study* (Junction City, Ore.: Eye Opener Publishers, 1967), p. 14.

43Wilson, *Scientific Investigation,* p. 69.

44*Ibid.,* p. 70.

45Unger, *Introductory Guide,* p. 158.

46Wilson, *Scientific Investigation,* p. 72.

47*Ibid.*

48Millar Burrows, *The Dead Sea Scrolls* (New York: The Viking Press, 1955), pp. 303-4.

49Wilson, *Scientific Investigation,* pp. 81-82.

50*Ibid.,* p. 85.

51*Ibid.,* p. 86.

52*Ibid.*

53John H. Skilton, "The Transmission of the Scriptures," *The Infallible Word,* ed. N. B. Stonehouse and Paul Woolley (3d rev. printing; Philadelphia: Presbyterian and Reformed Publishing Co., 1946), p. 159.

54J. Harold Greenlee, *Introduction to New Testament Textual Criticism* (Grand Rapids: William B. Eerdmans Publishing Co., 1964), p. 71.

55Zane C. Hodges, "Introduction to the *Textus Receptus"* (unpublished course notes, Greek 301, Dallas Theological Seminary, 1967), p. 1.

56*Ibid.*

57D. A. Thompson, "The Greek New Testament and the Modern Versions," *The Reformation Link,* 19 (December 1967): 20.

58*Ibid.,* pp. 20-21.

59*Ibid.,* p. 21.

60*Ibid.*

61Edward F. Hills, *The King James Version Defended* (Des Moines: The Christian Research Press, 1956), p. 119.

62*Ibid.*

63John Joseph Mangan, *Life, Character, and Influence of Desiderius Erasmus of Rotterdam* (New York: The Macmillan Co, 1927), p. 3.

64Frederick G. Kenyon, *Handbook to the Textual Criticism of the New Testament* (London: Macmillan and Co., Ltd., 1901), p. 227.

65*Ibid.*

66*Ibid.*

67Greenlee, *Introduction,* p. 70.

68Preserved Smith, *Erasmus* (New York and London: Harper and Row Publishers, 1923), pp. 164-65.

69*Ibid.,* p. 165.

70Kenyon, *Handbook,* ref. 64, p. 229.

71Zane C. Hodges, "The Ecclesiastical Text of Revelation — Does It Exist?" *Bibliotheca Sacra* 118 (1961): 113.

72Greenlee, *Introduction,* p. 80.

[73]Zane C. Hodges, "The Greek Text of the King James Version," *Bibliotheca Sacra* 125 (1968): 339.

[74]E. C. Colwell, "Scribal Habits in Early Papyri: A Study in the Corruption of the Text," *The Bible in Modern Scholarship*, ed. J. Philip Hyatt (Nashville: Abingdon Press, 1965), p. 383.

[75]Kurt Aland, "The Significance of the Papyri for Progress in New Testament Research," *The Bible in Modern Scholarship*, ed. J. Philip Hyatt (Nashville: Abingdon Press, 1965), p. 337.

[76]Hodges, "Greek Text," p. 341.

[77]Aland, "Significance," p. 333.

[78]Hodges, "Introduction," pp. 4-5.

[79]Kurt Aland, "The Greek New Testament: Its Present and Future Editions," *Journal of Biblical Literature* 87 (1968): 184.

[80]Hodges, "Greek Text," p. 335.

[81]Burgon, *Traditional Text*, p. 17.

[82]*Ibid.*

[83]Kurt Aland et al., eds., *The Greek New Testament* (Stuttgart, West Germany: Württemberg Bible Society, 1966), p. vii.

[84]Hodges, "Introduction," ref. 55, pp. 8-9.

[85]Hermann F. von Soden, *Die Schriften Des Neuen Testament* (3 vols.; Gottingen: Vandenhoeck und Ruprecht, 1911).

[86]Hodges, "Introduction," p. 9.

[87]Harry A. Sturz, "The Use of the Byzantine Text-type in New Testament Textual Criticism" (unpublished Th.D. dissertation, Grace Theological Seminary, 1967), p. 222.

[88]Westminster Confession of 1647, Chapter 7, Section VIII.

ALPHABETICAL
and
SCRIPTURAL
INDEXES

prepared by
Paul E. Gregg Jr.

ALPHABETICAL INDEX

A

SCRIPTURAL INDEX